That You May Know

A PRIMER ON CHRISTIAN DISCIPLESHIP

By Jacob D. Gerber

19Baskets

19Baskets, Inc.
3900 Old Cheney Rd., Ste. 201–225
Lincoln, NE 68516
http://19baskets.com

First Edition

Cover design by Lisa Moore. Photos used in cover by Alex Trukhin and Lacey Raper, licensed Creative Commons Zero.

Contents

Foreword

Whether you are a new believer or a seasoned saint, you will benefit greatly from reading this book. It does exactly what a Bible commentary should do—enlighten, encourage, and enrich—and it does so in a manner that is clear, wise, and practical.

I have heard the author preach many times and have appreciated the way he stays on track and avoids detours. His approach is practical, and he does not waste words or ignore difficulties. He explains God's truth clearly and applies the truth courageously.

I have been in ministry over sixty years, and I think I am correct in saying that Christians today desperately need the truths found in John's Epistles. John's teaching on truth, love, spiritual growth, prayer, and faith is exactly what we need. We have won many converts but have not made many disciples, and some of the disciples we have mentored have strayed from following the Master. If God's people take to heart the truths taught in First, Second, and Third John and obey them, it could mark the beginning of the spiritual awakening that many of us have been asking God to send.

As you read with your heart open to the Lord, He will speak to you through what His servant has written; and that could be the beginning of a new spiritual adventure for you.

Warren W. Wiersbe
Former Pastor – The Moody Church, Chicago

Acknowledgments

No book is a solo project, even when only one author has his name on the cover. I could not have written this book without the support of a number of people, so I want to extend to you my thanks.

Thank you to my wife, Allison, and my children, Evelyn and Zachariah. Allison, you supported and encouraged me through this process, listening to the original sermons that shaped this book, and even reading through my book to offer suggestions once it was written. Thank you so much for letting me take the time to finish this project—I know that it was a sacrifice at times, so thank you for everything. Evelyn and Zachariah, I love you both. Thanks for letting Dad work to get this completed!

Thank you to my parents who have supported me in so many ways for a long time, especially in my work and ministry. Your encouragement has been invaluable for my entire life, so thank you for everything you did for me and gave to me along the way. There is no way that I would be where I am without you.

Thank you to the team from Lincoln Berean College Group with whom I studied 1 John for the first time back in 2005. My love for the letters of John began in our meetings at the Mill in downtown Lincoln, so thank you to Matt and Renee Meyer, Andrew Osten, Dan Brown, and Ben Zuehlke. The work we did in writing a Bible study for Real Time are some of my fondest memories from college.

Thank you to the churches where I preached from the letters of John, including Lincoln Berean Church (Lincoln,

NE), Crete Berean Church (Crete, NE), First Evangelical Covenant Church (Lincoln, NE), Redeemer Church (Lincoln, NE), Ebenezer Congregational Church (Lincoln, NE), Harvest Community Church (Omaha, NE), and Steadfast Bible Fellowship (Omaha, NE). It was a delight to open God's word with you, and God used those times to teach me 1, 2, and 3 John in ways that prepared me to write this book.

Thank you to my editor, Renae Morehead, who so carefully combed through my manuscript to raise helpful questions, smooth out awkward phrases, align styles, and cut out the absurd amount of italics I wanted to use. Every time I accepted your suggested changes, I could feel my book becoming that much better because of your help. I cannot thank you enough for your work.

Thank you to my friends who read my manuscript and offered extremely helpful advice, comments, and questions: Gerald Bray, Parker Johnson, Vern Steiner, Hope Blanton, Terence Waldron, Andrew Hansen, Derek Jacks, Jake Hanson, Cary Hughes, and Judd Spencer.

Thank you especially to Warren Wiersbe for not only offering advice and suggestions for the book (especially the suggestion to add chapters on 2 John and 3 John), but for writing the foreword to this book. I greatly admire your own writing and publishing, so having you write the foreword is something I will always treasure.

Thank you to Lisa Moore for using your incredible design talents to put a top-notch cover on this book. People will always judge books by their covers, so thank you for making a cover that I can be proud of.

Finally, I want to thank everyone who contributed to my Kickstarter campaign to raise money for editing, designing, and laying out the text of this book. I would not have had the resources to get this book finished apart from your generous support, so thank you to the following people: Terry and Becky Gerber, the Price-Williams family, Ryan and Leisha Pitkin, Rev. Anthony and Stacy Gerber, Brad and Nancy

Brestel, Grant Heilman, Marc and Kerri Koenig, John and Carla Watson, Dave and Tanya Bydalek, Dan and Blythe Hawthorne, Beth Haase, Jake Hanson, Christian and Wendy Ledesma, Larry and Susie Carlson, Sherri Erickson, Jared and Tiffany Wadell, Mark Schwarting and Cathy Nelson, A. Evan Westburg, Vicki Halstrom, Dale and Susan Miller, Dana Danielson, Andrew and Allissa DeBoer, Marc Koenig, Austin and Tara Mackrill, Jared, McKenzie, and Ashton Clough, Tim and Amy Lockwood, J. Norfleete Day, Lisa Moore, Ann Iona Warner, David Reitman, Lucas Hains, Chris Plucker, Jon Curlee, Jesse and Laura Dotterer, Dr. Patricia Bridewell, Bob and Iris Johnson, Chris Davis, Terence Waldron, Ina Sivits Luhring, Tom and Debbie Wagner, Dennis and Charlotte Carlson, Ryan and Jackie Cech, Brian and Beth Staswick, Lindsey Friesen, Don and Karen Friesen, Tim and Jane Erickson, Curtis W. Stutzman, Benjamin J. Keele, Mark and Jill Haw, Steve and Angelique Curtis, Parker Johnson, Ron Jacobson, Robert Seeger, Dan, Katie, Clara, and Ethan Mattix, Jason "Swan" Martin, David and Jamie Watson, Viacheslav Myachin, Daniel J. Lehman, Theodore Rogers, Adam S. Berry, Angela Bardot, Jason Loh, Charlotte Custer, Merle and Kay Brestel, Marlene Bechtold, and Brandon and Michaela Mueller.

A Note on
Bible Translations in
This Book

U nless otherwise noted, all the Bible passages in this book are taken from the English Standard Version (ESV). The only exception is that all the unmarked passages from 1, 2, and 3 John are my own translation. So, in the places where I have used the ESV's translation of John's letters, those passages are marked with the label "ESV."

In my own translations of 1, 2, and 3 John, I have tried to stay as literally close to the original Greek text as possible, especially to make some of the nuances clearer that I talk about in my exposition of the passages. This makes my translation rougher than most translations you will find, but it helps to get to the clear meaning of the passage. So, if I need to supply a word that doesn't actually exist to make sense of a passage, that word appears in italics.

On the other hand, if a purely literal translation would have resulted in English gibberish, I smoothed the translation out just enough to make it readable while sacrificing as little of the original sense as possible. This isn't really a translation meant for in-depth exegetical work, and it probably isn't ideal for normal reading. Instead, it's a translation written to help cast light on the nuances of what John is teaching us about discipleship in these letters.

Introduction

When Jesus describes the kind of relationship that he wants to have with us, he says, "Come, follow me." This is what he said to his first group of disciples, and this is still what he tells those of us who would be his disciples today. That is what it means to be a disciple—to follow him wherever he leads us by learning from him, enjoying his presence, and obeying what he teaches us along the way.

Over the last two thousand years, Christians have written countless books on the subject of discipleship. A few of these books have become enduring classics that continue to be read even hundreds of years after they were originally published, but countless discipleship books fade quickly into obscurity, largely because there are so many other options available. At this point, don't we have enough resources on discipleship? Why would I write yet another book on such a thoroughly explored topic, and why should you read it?

What makes this book unique is that I wrote it to teach about Christian discipleship through a close study of the Scriptures themselves. While there are many books about discipleship, there are not nearly enough that primarily expound the Bible. The best resources on discipleship always bring us back to God's word because following Jesus ultimately means that we need to learn directly from Jesus in his word.

The whole reason God spoke to us in the first place was so that we could come to know him as well as knowing "all things that pertain to life and godliness" (2 Peter 1:3). "All

Scripture," Paul writes, "is breathed out by God and profitable for teaching, for reproof, for correction, and for training in righteousness, that the man of God may be complete, equipped for every good work" (2 Timothy 3:16–17).

Indeed, all Scripture is profitable, but about nine years ago, I began learning just how powerful one portion of Scripture in particular was for teaching the essentials of Christian discipleship.

Nine years ago, I studied 1 John in-depth for the first time.

DISCIPLESHIP ACCORDING TO JOHN

I initially studied 1 John seriously in the fall of 2005, when I was part of a team who prepared a Bible study for all the small groups in my college ministry. I will always treasure my memories of that study time together as we pored over the text of 1 John.

Since then I have preached on various passages from the letters of John at seven different churches, preaching all the way through 1 John twice at two churches where I served as interim pastor. I have led several one-to-one Bible studies with individuals whom I had the privilege of discipling, and I even saw someone come to know Jesus for the first time during one of those individual studies. The book of 1 John is precious to me.

At some point along the way, I began to reflect on what the Apostle John tells us when he describes his purpose behind writing the letter in 1 John 5:13: "I write these things to you who believe in the name of the Son of God that you may know that you have eternal life" (ESV). What's so interesting about this verse is that John wrote something almost identical toward the end of his book we call the Gospel of John:

> [30]Now Jesus did many other signs in the presence of the disciples, which are not written in this book; [31]but these are written so that you may believe that Jesus is the Christ, the Son of God, and that by believing you

may have life in his name. (John 20:30–31)

John's first letter is written "to you who believe in the name of the Son of God," but the Gospel of John is written "so that you may believe that Jesus is the Christ, the Son of God." Additionally, 1 John is written "that you may know that you have eternal life," while the Gospel of John is written "that by believing you may have life in his name."

The best way to understand these two books, then, is to recognize John wrote his Gospel for the purpose of evangelism (to help people who don't know Christ to begin to know him) but that he then wrote his first letter for the purpose of discipleship (to help people who do know Christ to know him better). This doesn't mean that John's Gospel has nothing to offer to believers, or that 1 John cannot lead anyone to a saving knowledge of Christ—in fact, both of those ideas are absolutely false. Instead, this simply means that John had different primary purposes for writing each, and that the primary purpose of 1 John is for training disciples.

When I reflected on this, I began to ask, "So what did John do in 1 John for the sake of training disciples?" If someone published a new book on discipleship today, most of us would have a pretty good idea of what we might find inside the book, even if we never opened it. But what would a Holy Spirit-inspired apostle of the Lord Jesus include in his book about discipleship?

As I asked those questions, I began to see that John's letter is both simple and wide reaching. With deceptively easy writing (students studying Greek for the first time often begin by reading 1 John because the Greek is so simple), John focuses on four main topics: the righteousness of God, our own sin, the gospel of Jesus, and how we begin to live as obedient disciples as a result of the work of the gospel in our lives. John returns again and again to these same topics throughout the entire letter, building and developing, returning and reflecting, spiraling closer and closer toward the center of his message.

But even so, John never repeats himself. He says similar things along the way, but in each section of 1 John, the apostle looks at his core curriculum from a fresh angle. In this way, John covers a broad range of topics that every Christian, from the newest convert to the most seasoned saint, desperately needs: truth, gospel, growth, perseverance, hope, righteousness, discernment, love, faith, prayer, and eternal life. Then, he gives a practical demonstration of these topics through two case studies in 2 John and 3 John.

Sometimes, John teaches about deep theological issues, such as the incarnation of Jesus or the anointing of the Holy Spirit. Other times, he asks searchingly practical questions of how we are caring for the most vulnerable in our midst: "But if anyone has the world's goods and sees his brother in need, yet closes his heart against him, how does God's love abide in him?" (1 John 3:17 ESV). Everywhere, he writes warmly, with sensitive pastoral care and a deep passion for the glory of Jesus Christ, as well as a clear vision of the gospel:

> [1]My little children, I am writing these things to you so that you may not sin. But if anyone does sin, we have an advocate with the Father, Jesus Christ the righteous. [2]He is the propitiation for our sins, and not for ours only but also for the sins of the whole world. (1 John 2:1–2 ESV)

The letters of John are simple but complex. The youngest Christian will find these letters easily digestible, but John has actually provided a feast for all believers to return to again and again over the course of our discipleship journeys. I have been through 1 John several times over the last nine years, and I can tell you from my own experience that we will always find some new dish to taste that we had not yet discovered.

Gregory the Great (540–604) wrote, "Scripture is like a river again, broad and deep, shallow enough here for the lamb to go wading, but deep enough there for the elephant to swim."[1] Gregory wrote this sentence in his commentary on

Job, but it is often quoted today to describe the Gospel of John. Regardless of Gregory's original intent, his statement is absolutely true of 1, 2, and 3 John.

A PRIMER ON CHRISTIAN DISCIPLESHIP

This book is an exploration of what God teaches us about following Jesus through the writings of his beloved servant John. I cannot offer wildly new ideas or special insights into divine mysteries, and you should probably not trust me if I did! Instead, I can only claim that I have sought to follow the example of the many godly teachers who have gone before me by putting God's word on center stage so that we could all gaze together upon the glory of Jesus revealed there. It is my prayer that this book will help you to know Jesus better through his word, not that you would pay any particular attention to the book itself.

This book is also the first in what I hope will be a series of several studies of the Scriptures, which I am calling the Primer Series. I have already begun planning future volumes for this series that, God-willing, will share this vision for seeing and loving Jesus in and through his word.

But for now, let's open God's word together to the First Letter of John. May God pour out his Holy Spirit upon us to give us eyes to see, ears to hear, and hearts to understand all that is contained in the gospel of Jesus Christ.

1
Truth

1 John 1:1–4

For all the ways Jesus could have described our relationship to him, he chose to call us his "disciples." The Greek word we translate as "disciple" literally means "learner," which means that at the most basic level, following Jesus means learning more about him all the days of our lives. Being a disciple of Jesus means we are called to learn about his nature, his identity, his character, his great work of salvation, and his instructions for us.

The word *disciple* is closely related to the word *discipline*— not the angry discipline of a cranky teacher, but the discipline that an inspiring teacher, coach, or mentor helps us to achieve to pursue a goal. Just as the discipline of music, writing, painting, or sculpting is something that a disciple would spend a lifetime perfecting, so following Jesus is a lifelong journey to grow in our understanding, love, and faith in Jesus.

This also means that there are not any quick and easy ways of learning as disciples. Do you ever read a passage from the Bible that you don't understand? Do you ever deal with situations that you don't think a righteous God ought to have allowed? Do you ever stay up late into the night, praying to God for answers that never seem to come? If so, then you have shared in the common, agonizing, truth-seeking experience of every other follower of Jesus throughout history. Part of learning to follow Jesus means learning to trust that he is gracious, loving, and wise even when he chooses not to reveal to us all that we desire to know.

But at the end of the day, Christian truth is characterized not by agony but by joy—or, better, Christian truth is characterized by joy in the midst of agony. Even when following Jesus becomes especially hard, Jesus calls his disciples to continue trusting in him, believing that he is the only place we can find real truth that will satisfy and delight us throughout eternity. As Jesus' disciples, we cannot hedge our bets by looking for truth anywhere else—not because we ourselves have all the answers, but because we believe that Jesus does. Whether he chooses to answer a given question is not the point. Instead, Christian discipleship means recognizing that whatever truth we learn, we will learn it from him.

THE TRUTH OF CHRISTIANITY

At its core, Christianity is about truth. Even more, Christianity has nothing at all to offer if the whole thing is based on a lie. Beginning our study of discipleship here is critical, especially in a postmodern world that has redefined truth to be whatever anyone wants it to be. In fact, the Apostle Paul went so far as to say, "If in Christ we have hope in this life only, we are of all people most to be pitied" (1 Corinthians 15:19). If the hope we have beyond this life is a sham, then living for Jesus in this life is embarrassingly pathetic.

Some Christians have no problem believing that Christianity is truth. If they did not believe that Christianity was true, they could not be Christians. The issue is not complicated in their minds, and they would probably prefer to skip the subject of truth altogether and just move onto something else.

There are, however, three reasons why we still need to begin our study of discipleship with a study of truth. First, even those who believe in the truth of Christianity nevertheless still struggle to find truth in particular situations in their lives. Only superficial truth comes easily, and superficial truth cannot satisfy us for very long. If we really want life-giving, joy-in-the-midst-of-sorrow truth, we all need to grow roots that sink deeply into the truth of Jesus.

Second, we need to know how to talk to the people who do not think that Christianity needs to be true to be good or helpful. Some believe that Christianity is mainly about ethics so that Jesus' goal was primarily to teach us how to live good lives. Others believe that Christianity is merely a source of beauty, where we gain personal enrichment and fulfillment. Although Christianity does establish a system of ethics, and although Christianity is a source of beauty, it is more than those things because Christianity is true. But if Christianity is not true, then it cannot be ethical, beautiful, or even good in any way at all. If Christianity is false, then we are fools to pursue it any further.

Third, we need to know how to talk to people who reject the truth of Christianity altogether. Many people do not see beauty in Jesus at all, and they see oppression and bigotry in Christianity rather than ethical righteousness and holiness. Nevertheless, Jesus gave an ongoing commission to his disciples, commanding us to make new disciples from all the nations (Matthew 28:18–20), and that Great Commission requires that we understand how to proclaim the truth of Jesus to those who do not yet believe.

And so, in the opening words of the First Letter of John, the author wastes no time to anchor all that he wants to say in truth—a truth he has personally experienced. He writes:

> ¹What was from *the* beginning, what we have heard, what we have seen with our eyes, what we have looked upon and our hands have touched concerning the word of life—²and the life was manifested, and we have seen and we bear witness and we declare to you the eternal life, who was toward the Father and was manifested to us. (1 John 1:1–2)

John seems almost to struggle putting together words that can accurately capture the overwhelming truth of Christianity.

These verses (along with verse 3) make up a lengthy run-on sentence in the original Greek as John tries to summarize this truth. He begins with three aspects of the truth.

TRUTH IS FROM THE BEGINNING

First, John tells us that the truth is "from the beginning," which means that the truth is absolute, unchangeable, fixed, eternal, unshakable, and immovable. The truth is the same yesterday, today, and forever. No one can persuade, bully, coerce, push, or change the truth in even the smallest degree.

Christian discipleship means submitting to God's eternal truth and acknowledging the limitations of our own knowledge. We are new, but God's truth is from the beginning. We are brief, but God's truth endures forever. We are small, but God's truth is big. We are constantly changing, but God's truth remains the same. The path of discipleship leads us to distrust ourselves while increasingly trusting in God's truth.

THE LIFE WAS MANIFESTED

Second, John testifies that this truth was put on display among us in a very real, tangible, sensible way as a "life... manifested," so that John and the other apostles listened to the truth speak, gazed upon the truth with their eyes, and even touched the truth with their hands. This truth is not a pie-in-the-sky abstraction invented by a manipulative con artist to gain power over the weak-minded. Some people will believe any strange idea that a cult leader teaches, but that is not what is happening here. John is not telling us about a floaty, other-worldly idea that came to him in some dream; he is giving us an eyewitness account of someone with whom he personally walked and talked.

John is describing a man—a flesh-and-blood human being, just like you and me. John says that he heard this man speak. He saw this man with his own eyes—in fact, he gazed upon this man long enough to know that this man was a human being, and not just someone who only seemed to be

4

human. And John is even telling us here that he touched this person with his own hands. This was no angel or ghost or mystical vision in the night—this was a man like us, who lived in our midst.

TRUTH IS A PERSON

Third, John finally identifies this truth. At this point, he knows we are still wondering, What is this truth of Christianity? In what exactly are we putting our confidence and trust? John makes it clear very quickly that when he talks about truth, he is not proclaiming the bizarre teachings of a cult nor a watered-down truth that simply encourages us to be good people. Instead, John points us to something extraordinary, yet practical: truth is not merely a doctrine but a person.

The most intriguing way that John describes this personal relationship between God and the truth is when he writes that this truth was *toward* the Father. Most Bible translations use the word *with* the Father, but the Greek word John selected is not one of the normal words for "with" (*sun* or *meta*) but the word *pros*, which is related to the word *prosopon*, the Greek word for "face." The Greek word *pros* works almost exactly the way our English language would describe two objects as "facing" each other when they are positioned "toward" each other.

R. C. H. Lenski (1864–1936) explains the effect of using the word *toward* instead of *with* suggests "living relationship, intimate converse."[1] The Father did not know the truth in a purely intellectual, dry way, but the Father actually had some kind of intimate, face-to-face relationship with the truth!

To understand what John is telling us about the personal nature of this truth, it is important to see the many similarities between 1 John 1:1–2 and the opening verses of the Apostle John's Gospel. Compare:

1 John 1:1: What was from the beginning...
John 1:1: In the beginning was the Word...

1 John 1:1: ...what we have seen with our eyes...
John 1:14: ...and we have seen his glory...

1 John 1:2: ...the life was manifested...
John 1:4: In him was life, and the life was the light of men.

1 John 1:2: who was toward [*pros*] the Father...
John 1:1, 2: ...and the Word was with [*pros*] God... He was in the beginning with God.[2]

1 John 1:2: ...and was manifested to us...
John 1:14: And the Word became flesh and dwelt among us...

Clearly, the "word of life" in the First Letter of John is the same "Word made flesh" from John's Gospel: in both places, John is bearing witness to the person of the Lord Jesus Christ! This Jesus is the eternal Son who has been in face-to-face fellowship with the Father from the beginning but who now has been manifested among us as a human being.

This person is the greatest truth that John experienced in his entire life. As John and the other disciples lived in the presence of Jesus, traveling with him, eating and drinking with him, listening to him, and watching him interact with people and with God, they slowly came to understand the identity of their teacher: this man is also God!

The central message of Christianity is that God manifested his truth to us not through science, philosophy, or art (i.e., through human efforts to reach up to God's truth) but rather by sending his Son down to us to become a fellow human being alongside of us. Whatever else Christianity is, John wants us to know first and foremost that Christianity is about God's gracious choice to manifest in our midst the truth of the person Jesus Christ, the eternal God who became man.

THE FELLOWSHIP OF CHRISTIANITY

Because truth is a person, the truth of Jesus Christ is more than just a set of facts. This truth carries important implications that should change the way we live our lives. Specifically, John tells us that the truth of Jesus Christ leads to fellowship in two directions—fellowship within the church and fellowship with the Father and the Son. Put another way, John is telling us that truth is personal.

John continues the run-on sentence that begins his first letter in verses 3 and 4:

> [3]what we have seen and have heard, we bear witness also to you, that also you may have fellowship with us. And our fellowship *is* with the Father and with his Son Jesus Christ. [4]And these things we write, that our joy may be filled.

Fellowship means a relational commonality, or something actively shared between those in relationship with one another. John's description of fellowship, then, is a bit surprising. He explains that his goal in writing is "that also you may have fellowship with us. And our fellowship is with the Father and with his Son Jesus Christ." Why is John's first goal "that also you may have fellowship *with us*"? Why not allow his readers immediate fellowship with the Father and the Son? Why must we have fellowship with John and the apostles first? There are two issues here.

On the one hand, John is not describing a purely institutional fellowship. In other words, he is not urging people toward bare church membership, as though we could be saved simply by making sure to jump through the hoops of joining a church or of making a point of attending the majority of that church's worship services. Joining a church is important and should never be neglected by anyone serious about following Jesus, but it is Jesus alone who saves and not church membership. As George Smeaton (1814–89) writes, "It is the believer's relation to Christ that puts him in connection with the Church; not his connection with the Church that puts him into a saving relation to Christ."[3] John is suggesting nothing to the contrary.

To underscore the fact that Jesus alone saves, consider all the places in 1 John where the apostle speaks of salvation or condemnation (e.g., 1:9; 2:1–2, 22–23; 3:23–24; 4:2–3; 5:4–13, 20–21). In each of these texts, the issue at stake is always whether or not we believe in or reject Jesus as the Christ, the Son of God having-come-in-flesh, the one true God who is eternal life. John is not so much pointing to the people or to the institution as he is insisting upon fellowship (relational commonality) with the apostles regarding the truth of Jesus.

The fellowship "with us" that John writes about, then, is our common faith in the Lord Jesus Christ, the witness of the apostles concerning the Word of Life who was manifested in their midst. Of course, we must have fellowship with the apostles to join in their fellowship with the Father and the Son—we know nothing about the Father and the Son apart from what they have taught us.

On the other hand, there is a growing tendency among Christians (especially American evangelical Christians) to look upon the institution of the church with some disdain, preferring to take a me-and-Jesus-only approach. The radical individualism of American culture has raised a crop of Christians who embrace Jesus (at least, their own version of Jesus) but who reject the church filled with the other sinners whom Jesus came to save.

Of course, this is understandable to a certain degree. Jesus is perfect; his church is not. Jesus gave his very life that we might live; people in the church can sometimes defend all manner of selfishness and egotism in the name of God. But Christ has not given us the option of embracing himself while rejecting his church. One early Christian theologian named Cyprian of Carthage (200–258) put it bluntly: "You cannot have God for your Father if you have not the church for your Mother."[4]

Again, it isn't that bare membership in a church can save you; only Jesus can save. Still, when Christ saves us, he doesn't bring us to himself as loosely connected individuals, where each person is connected to Jesus on an individual, one-to-one basis. Instead, he saves us to integrate us all together into his church. We do not have the choice between Christ and the church. Christ died to save his church, and if we are indeed servants of Jesus, then we will love Jesus' church. If you wish to have fellowship with the Father and with his Son Jesus Christ, you must have fellowship with the church that the Father sent his Son to die for.

But the good news is that God loves his church, and he works uniquely in and through his church to bring truth to his church, first to lead us to salvation and then to teach us for the rest of our lives what it means to follow Jesus day after day. In the church, God sends his Holy Spirit to bring life to dead men, women, and children. In the church, God pours out his Holy Spirit to open up to us the meaning of the Scriptures to convict us of our sin and to grant us the repentance and faith necessary for salvation. In the church, God's Holy Spirit teaches us everything about the glory of the crucified and resurrected Lord Jesus Christ, who is himself true God and eternal life—and whoever confesses the Son has the Father also (1 John 2:23).

God doesn't give us the fullness of his truth in a vacuum, where we are isolated and on our own. God's truth is a person, and he only gives us the fullness of his truth through our personal relationships with the others in the church whom he is saving. In this fellowship of the church, by the Holy Spirit, the Father grants us full access to himself through the truth of his Son Jesus Christ.

So, we begin our study of discipleship here, with the truth who is a person, Jesus Christ. John is urging us to make his joy complete by embracing the eyewitness testimony of the apostles concerning the truth—that is, concerning the Word of Life manifested—so that we can have fellowship together; and indeed our fellowship is with the Father and with his Son Jesus Christ.

QUESTIONS FOR REFLECTION

1. When we think and talk about truth, are we thinking and talking about a person? What would change in our thinking, speaking, and living if we were?
2. The Apostle John balances the necessity of every individual's faith with the necessity of fellowship with the larger church. Do you emphasize one side over the other? What would need to change practically in your life if you struck a more biblical balance?

2
Gospel

1 John 1:5–2:6

W hen I was in high school, our teachers and
administrators organized a full week of events
and activities designed to raise awareness about
the dangers of drunk driving. One afternoon we were
all dismissed from our normal classes so that we could
participate in several activities to emphasize the dangers of
driving drunk. The most interesting of these activities was
the "drunk goggles." These goggles had special lenses that
impaired our spatial reasoning, making it difficult to judge
the distance from us to the things around us. The goggles
made it hard to walk and impossible to shoot a basketball
successfully. We all took turns driving a car slowly through
orange cones set up in the school's parking lot. We laughed
at how silly we all looked as we were unable to do very basic
things while wearing these glasses.

Now, for the moment, set aside the question of whether
the drunk goggles were actually teaching us how much fun it
was to have our vision and spatial reasoning impaired. (The
kids who seemed to enjoy the goggles most were the kids who
used to brag on Monday mornings about how drunk they got
over the weekends.) The important point for our purposes
is that these goggles provide a picture of how sin affects our
perception of reality. Sin distorts and twists our ability to see

ourselves, others, and even God correctly. As long as we wear "sin goggles," we will never see things as they truly are.

John writes in this next section to clarify our vision with the meaning and importance of the gospel. In other words, he writes to remove the sin goggles from our eyes. John focuses specifically on the ways that sin distorts our understanding of reality, and he reorients us to see accurately who God is, who we are, and what our sin has made us in the sight of God. Then, he corrects two extremes in the way we mistakenly try to deal with our sinfulness. Pay careful attention to this passage, because if we miss John's message about the gospel, our journey as disciples of Jesus will stall out before we even get started.

GOD IS LIGHT

In 1 John 1:5, John writes:

> And this is the message that we have heard from him and proclaim to you, that God is light, and darkness is not in him, not at all.

John begins this passage about the gospel with such a seemingly simple statement that at first we are tempted to read over it quickly to get to something a little more thought-provoking. John, though, is a master of deceptively simple language that the smallest child can understand at once and that a great theologian can spend a lifetime pondering.

The meaning of this sentence turns largely on the meaning of a single word that John uses here in verse 5. When he says, "And this is the *message* that we have heard from him and proclaim to you," he is using the Greek word *angellia*, a word that means "message" or "news." If you add to this word the prefix *eu*–, which means "good," you get *euangellion*, or "good news," and that word for "good news" is the word our English Bibles frequently translate as "gospel."

So, in 1 John 1:5, John is giving us news, but it is not good news. In fact, the news John gives us is actually very bad news, but more on that in a moment. This is the news that John gives to us: "God is light, and darkness is not in him, not at all." Literally, John is using a double negative to convey the strength of what he is saying: God is light, and in him is *no* darkness—*none* at all.

Now, why should we think the message that God is light is bad news? After all, who would ever want to serve and worship a god in whom there was darkness? That is, why would we prefer a god who was cruel, hateful, and evil? Shouldn't we be thrilled that God's character is light (kindness, love, and goodness) so that in him there is not one speck of darkness whatsoever?

Taken by itself, it is a very good thing that God is light, and that in him there is no darkness at all. The problem, then, is not with God but with *us* and with our own relationship to this God-who-is-light. You see, if God is light, then he cannot tolerate the darkness in which *we* live. God's holiness is not the problem. Our sinfulness is the problem.

Here's the point: If God is light, but we walk in darkness, then we cannot have any commonality (fellowship) with God. And, if we can have no commonality with God, then we have no hope in this life or the next. This news means that we are cut off forever from the God-who-is-light. John's message is bad news indeed.

But before moving on to other news—good news—John insists that we begin here, right at this point. John wants us to pause at this verse and think about the darkness in our lives, as compared to the perfection of God's light. He wants us to come fully to terms with our own sin, our guilt, and our hopelessness—the bad news—before he tells us the rest of the story of what God has done to rescue us from our darkness. You see, we cannot recognize the gospel as good news unless we recognize just how bad our condition is.

So, before we move on in this chapter, ask yourself whether you have genuinely come to recognize your need of Jesus. Have you fully appreciated the radiant, blazing holiness of God, and have you identified the darkness of your own guilt as you stand before him? Do you realize that you actually deserve God's holy wrath against your sin? Have you completely despaired of your own ability to stand confidently before God on the Day of Judgment?

Or, are you wearing sin goggles that make it impossible to see the reality of your darkness in contrast to the God-who-is-light, in whom there is not a speck of darkness whatsoever?

If you do not acknowledge your darkness, then you do not yet understand the nature of Christian discipleship. Following Jesus requires us to acknowledge and confess our sins before God, and until we stand fully exposed in the light of God's holiness and recognize how far short of the glory of God we fall, we cannot begin down the path of the gospel. Meditate on 1 John 1:5 and pray that God would give you eyes to see the light of his holiness and the darkness of your sin.

But if you do recognize your desperate need for salvation, then you are exactly where you need to be for now. Keep reading. John has better news coming.

REFORMING THE SPEECH
OF LEGALISTIC PHARISEES (LIKE ME)

If 1 John 1:5 is the bad news of Christianity, then John turns in the next few verses toward announcing the good news of Christianity, but he does so by challenging those who continue to deny their need for salvation. John writes:

> ⁶If we say that we have fellowship with him but we walk in darkness, we lie and do not practice the truth. ⁷But if we walk in the light just as he is in the light, we have fellowship with one another and the blood of Jesus his Son cleanses us from all sin. ⁸If we say that we do not have sin, we deceive ourselves, and the truth is not in us. ⁹If we confess our sins, faithful he is and just, that he will forgive us *our* sins and cleanse us from all unrighteousness. ¹⁰If we say that we have not sinned, we

make him a liar, and his word is not in us. (1 John 1:6–10)

THE LEGALIST LIE

Notice in these verses that John addresses the speech of those who say they have no sin (and, therefore, no need for salvation) three times:

1:6: If we say that we have fellowship with him [a relationship that requires sinlessness, since God himself is light] but we walk in darkness, we lie and do not practice the truth.

1:8: If we say that we do not have sin, we deceive ourselves, and the truth is not in us.

1:10: If we say that we have not sinned, we make him a liar, and his word is not in us.

Those who claim to be sinless deny the truth about themselves, and such a lie becomes an expanding deception. First, John explains that we simply "lie and do not practice the truth" (1:6). Second, we begin to "deceive ourselves, and the truth is not in us" (1:8). Take special note of verse 8: at some point, we become so skilled at lying about our sin that we deceive even ourselves! Third (and worst of all), we become so deluded by our own sin that we actually go so far as to accuse God of lying about our sin in the first place so that "we make him a liar," as though God were a corrupt judge (1:10).

So, the more we say we do not have sin, the more our lies get out of hand. Ultimately, if we continue to lie about having no sin in our lives, we come to the point where we will stop at nothing—not even outright blasphemy against God himself—to uphold our deceit.

In this passage, John is fighting the same battle Jesus did against the Pharisees (the religious leaders of the day): legalism. Legalism is the attempt to justify ourselves before God (and other people) by claiming to have done everything required of us—in other words, by claiming to have kept the law perfectly. Legalism is a kind of spiritual one-upmanship,

15

so it creates self-righteousness and pride in our hearts as we boast about how much better we have obeyed the law (whether God's law, our own, or someone else's) compared to everyone else.

The truth, though, is that all of us have sinned. When we claim to be without sin, we deceive others and even ourselves. This is exactly what the Pharisees did by boasting in their ability to keep God's commandments. When they were able to keep the law (at least, according to their own standards of obedience), they made a big show of doing so, demonstrating to everyone around them just how holy and righteous they were. But whenever they were not able to keep the law, they hid their failures from public view and justified their lapses in their own minds so that they could continue thinking of themselves as better than everyone else.

To keep us from following in their footsteps, Jesus gave this surprising warning:

> [19]Therefore whoever relaxes one of the least of these commandments and teaches others to do the same will be called least in the kingdom of heaven, but whoever does them and teaches them will be called great in the kingdom of heaven. [20]For I tell you, unless your righteousness exceeds that of the scribes and Pharisees, you will never enter the kingdom of heaven. (Matthew 5:19–20)

Jesus doesn't oppose legalism because he wants to set the bar lower but because he wants to set the bar higher, at the level of absolute, perfect obedience. If God is light, and if in him there is no darkness whatsoever, even the smallest faltering in our lives completely disqualifies us from enjoying the presence of God in eternity. If our righteousness does not infinitely exceed even the most righteous people on the planet, we will never enter the kingdom of heaven.

But additionally, Jesus opposed legalism because efforts to justify ourselves by keeping God's law undermine the whole purpose that God gave the law in the first place. God did not give the law so that we could spend our lifetimes showing others just what good people we are, and God especially did not give his laws as weapons to prove our superiority over others.

Instead, God gave us his law to teach us to love him and to love other people. When someone asked Jesus about the most important commandment, Jesus was very clear:

> [37]And he said to him, "You shall love the Lord your God with all your heart and with all your soul and with all your mind. [38]This is the great and first commandment. [39]And a second is like it: You shall love your neighbor as yourself. [40]On these two commandments depend all the Law and the Prophets. (Matthew 22:37–40)

The two commandments to love God and to love people summarize the purpose and intent of the entire law. By definition, you cannot fulfill the law when you use it to exalt yourself and to belittle others.

For the Pharisees, legalism caused them to look with contempt on everyone who was not as righteous as they were, and legalism eventually drove them to hate Jesus (the only man who was genuinely righteous) so much that they wrongfully demanded his execution. Even today, legalism continues to alienate us both from God and from other people.

THE GOSPEL FOR LEGALISTS

And yet, God shows mercy even to legalists. Just as Jesus extended the promises of the gospel to Pharisees like Nicodemus and Saul (who later became the Apostle Paul), so Jesus extends the promises of the gospel to self–righteous people like me and like you.

In 1 John 1:6–10, John carefully explains the gospel to legalists. He declares, You need to change your speech! Instead of saying that you are without sin (old speech), start to confess (new speech) the sin that you have: "If we confess our sins, faithful he is and just that he will forgive us our sins

17

and cleanse us from all unrighteousness" (1:9). Stop denying the truth, and start acknowledging the darkness in your life.

God is absolutely holy and righteous, so he does not allow us simply to ignore our sins. God would be unjust to turn a blind eye to our sin and allow injustice to remain in the world unchecked. So, instead of compounding our sin by lying about it, John tells us to confess our sins so that we can find forgiveness.

My own story is that of a reformed legalist. When I was growing up in the church, I always wanted to be known as "the good kid." My whole identity was based around the false idea that I was better than everybody else. So, I have struggled my entire life with the temptation to hide my sin from others. I want people to think that I am without sin, no matter how much I have to lie to keep up that facade.

The good news of the gospel, however, cuts through all of my deception. If I cannot humble myself to acknowledge my sinfulness, I am not merely lying, but I am actually refusing the forgiveness, cleansing, and righteousness that is mine in Jesus Christ! May God have mercy on our prideful hearts, because it is only through humbly confessing our sins that God promises true righteousness as he washes us clean by the cleansing blood of Jesus Christ.

HOW CAN GOD BE FAITHFUL AND JUST?

Now, let's pause for a moment. How can it be true that God will actually forgive our sins and cleanse us from all unrighteousness as long as we simply confess to our sins? Justice never works that way. The child still gets punished when she confesses to her parents about breaking the china that she wasn't supposed to touch. The criminal still goes to jail when he confesses to a burglary. Certainly, confession often lightens a punishment because no additional consequences for lying are added on top of the consequences for the crime itself, but justice always requires sin to be punished. On what basis, then, can God forgive our sins?

When I was young, I memorized 1 John 1:9: "If we confess our sins, he is faithful and just to forgive us our sins and to cleanse us from all unrighteousness" (ESV). From early on, this verse became an important part of my understanding of the gospel. God forgives us when we confess our sins to him.

Later, this verse took on new importance to me as I first began to study Greek in seminary and realized that our English translations have altered the word order. In the original language, John goes out of his way to emphasize God's faithfulness to forgive us, while still affirming God's righteousness, by writing, "Faithful he is and just." There have been moments in my life when I have despaired over my sin and have drawn great comfort from God's promise that he would be faithful to forgive me of my sin and to cleanse me of my unrighteousness.

Then, at some point along the way, I realized that I had always read right over the word *just*. The word *dikaios* is a Greek word that the English language translates into two words, depending on the context: "righteous" or "just." We typically say that a person is righteous, while a thing (whether a decision, a system, a country, a religion, etc.) is just. In Greek, the one word *dikaios* covers that entire range of meaning. So, the point here in 1 John 1:9 is that God is not only faithful to forgive us and cleanse us but that he is also just/righteous to do so.

This gets us back to our dilemma. How can God possibly be just/righteous when he subverts justice by refusing to punish anyone who merely confesses their sins? If a human judge in a court regularly pardoned the guilty for any reason at all, we would rightly call that judge corrupt and unjust, no matter what their reasons were for doing so (personal ties, bribery, extortion). How can we call God just/righteous for doing the same thing?

John feels the weight of this problem himself. Remember he opens this section of his letter with the message he heard from Jesus himself: "God is light, and darkness is not in him, not at all." Above all other considerations, God's perfect, pure holiness and righteousness must never be compromised, because God is light. He simply cannot allow darkness of any kind into his presence.

So how can God be faithful to forgive us, and yet still remain just? How can God cleanse sinners who walk in darkness so that we can walk with him in the pure light? This is a big challenge: If God cannot be faithful to forgive, then there is no gospel. If God cannot be just when he forgives, then the gospel is no longer good news. Who would ever want to live eternally with a corrupt God?

God solved this dilemma at the cross. There, God's perfect faithfulness and perfect justice came together in a bleeding, dying man: God's own Son Jesus Christ. At the cross, God poured out his wrath for our sin, but he poured it out on Jesus instead of on us. In this way, absolute justice has already been served and God remains just/righteous when he forgives sinners. At the cross, Jesus died for us so that God can now be faithful to forgive us our sins and to cleanse us from all unrighteousness without betraying his perfect purity.

This is why John writes in verse 7, "But if we walk in the light just as he is in the light, we have fellowship with one another *and the blood of Jesus his Son cleanses us from all sin.*" When we walk in the light (i.e., when we do not hide our sin but bring it into God's holy light through confession), God forgives us and cleanses us with the blood of Jesus.

I love this verse from John Newton's hymn "Let Us Love and Sing and Wonder":

Let us wonder; Grace and Justice
Join and point to mercy's store;
When through Grace in Christ our trust is,
Justice smiles and asks no more:
He Who washed us with His blood
Has secured our way to God.

Justice demands punishment for crime, while Grace longs to extend faithful forgiveness. While these two ought to oppose each other, they join together in urging us to look to Jesus, who secured our way to God with his own blood. He

who washed us with his blood has enabled God to be just/
righteous and the justifier (the one who faithfully makes us
righteous/justified) of the one who has faith in Jesus (Romans
3:26).

That gospel is *good* news.

REFORMING THE LIVES OF LAWLESS LIBERTINES (LIKE ME)

Legalism, however, is not the only extreme error that people
commit as they rebel against the gospel. In 1 John 2:1–6,
John turns his attention away from the speech of pharisaical
legalists, and he now targets the lives of lawless libertines.[1]
For the moment, we will skip 1 John 2:1–2 because it is helpful
to figure out the problem John is addressing (verses 3–6) in
order to understand the solution he offers (verses 1–2). So, in
verses 3 to 6, John writes:

> [3]And in this we know that we have come to know him,
> if we keep his commandments. [4]The one who says
> that "I have come to know him" but is not keeping his
> commandments, he is a liar and the truth is not in
> him. [5]Whoever keeps his word, truly in this one the
> love of God has been perfected. In this we know that
> we are in him. [6]The one who says he abides in him
> ought also to walk just as that one walked.

THE LIBERTINE LIE

The people John focuses on in this passage are those
who claim to know God but who do not think that they are
bound to keeping God's commandments. The attitude of the
libertines is the opposite of the attitude of the legalist. Where
legalists want to prove their right standing with God on the
basis of how well they keep the law, libertines insist that,
since they know God, they are under no obligation to keep
God's commandments whatsoever! In 1 John 1:6–10, John
confronted the lie of the legalists, and here, John unmasks
the lie of the libertines.

21

The problem with the libertines is often that they do not understand just how much God loves his own law. In fact, many libertines actually misuse New Testament discussions about the law by going so far as to suggest that the law itself is somehow bad. Certainly, efforts to justify ourselves by the law are bad, but God's law is perfectly good. Jesus was very clear: "Do not think that I have come to abolish the Law or the Prophets; I have not come to abolish them but to fulfill them" (Matthew 5:17). Even the Apostle Paul wrote, "Now we know that the law is good, if one uses it lawfully" (1 Timothy 1:8).

In fact, God's law is a perfect description of God's own character. So, if you want to know what God loves and what he hates, study the law. The Pharisees were dead wrong about how and why they should obey the law, but they were right to insist that God wanted his law to be taken seriously. They did not understand that our righteousness comes not by keeping the law but rather by faith in Jesus, whose blood cleanses us from unrighteousness and who himself fulfilled the law for us. We are righteous because Jesus was the perfect law-keeper who gives us his own righteousness through faith.

So, faith alone in Jesus alone is what saves us; however, saving faith is never alone. If we have indeed come to a saving faith in Jesus Christ, our lives will also begin to bear the fruit of good works. We will still fail (continuing to need the blood of Jesus to cleanse us), and every bit of our obedience will happen by nothing less than the grace of God, but in saving us, God gives us new hearts that desire to obey him.

We will look at this subject more in the next chapter, but for now, remember what Jesus told us: "If you love me, you will keep my commandments" (John 14:15). We simply do not have the option of ignoring Jesus' commandments. If we do not keep his commandments, then we reveal that we do not really love him. John means it when he says, "The one who says he abides in him ought also to walk just as that one [i.e., Jesus] walked" (1 John 2:6).

Ultimately, legalists and libertines alike fundamentally misunderstand the gospel because both groups do not grasp the significance of 1 John 1:5: "And this is the message that we have heard from him and proclaim to you, that God is light, and darkness is not in him, not at all." If God is perfect, pure, holy light, in whom there is no darkness at all, then he hates when we lie about the presence of sin in our lives (legalists). But by the same token, God hates it when we refuse to obey what he has commanded us (libertines). John states plainly, "The one who says that 'I have come to know him' but is not keeping his commandments, he is a liar and the truth is not in him" (1 John 2:4). For the disciple of Jesus Christ, neither option is acceptable.

THE GOSPEL FOR LIBERTINES

It is important to see, though, that John's message to libertines is not that they should swing the pendulum wildly back toward the law. Instead, John's solution is to reorient us to the gospel. In verses 1 and 2, he writes:

> ¹My little children, I am writing these things to you in order that you might not sin. But if someone sins, we have an advocate toward [*pros*] the Father, Jesus Christ the Righteous. ²And he is the propitiation concerning our sin, not concerning ours only, but also concerning the whole world.

One of the ways God uses the law is to show us our sin and the extent to which we fall short of the glory of God. Additionally, as we discussed earlier, God uses the law in the lives of believers to teach us about what he loves and what he hates so that we learn the character of God from the law. But the law is never the solution to our sinfulness—the law points us away from itself toward our solution.

To people whose lives are rotting away under sin, John counsels us to look not to the law but to our advocate, Jesus Christ the Righteous. As our righteous advocate, Jesus pleads on our behalf face-to-face [*pros*] with the Father, even as he calls us to deeper faith and obedience. John does not minimize the problem of sin—he is writing these things so that we may not sin!—but he points us to the gospel of Jesus Christ and not to the law as the solution.

The Scottish pastor Robert Murray M'Cheyne (1813–43) affirmed this idea in a letter to George Shaw, written in 1840: "Learn much of the Lord Jesus. For every look at yourself, take ten looks at Christ. He is altogether lovely. Such infinite majesty, and yet such meekness and grace and all for sinners, even the chief."[2] Whether we struggle with self–righteous legalism or libertine antinomianism, following Jesus means learning to look toward Christ alone for our salvation through faith. The law cannot save us, but the law is still good, so we must never try to get rid of it completely. The only way we can navigate through the twin demons of legalism on the one side and libertinism on the other is through the gospel of Jesus Christ, our advocate, whose blood cleanses us from all unrighteousness.

The more we look to ourselves (whether to our own abilities to keep the law or to our own desires that run contrary to the law), the more quickly we abandon the path of following Jesus toward holiness. So, for every look at yourself, take ten looks at Christ! The more we learn to enjoy the beauty of Christ through the eyes of faith, the more detestable our sin becomes to us, the more we cling to our advocate for righteousness, and the more we obey God's commandments by the power of the gospel in our lives.

QUESTIONS FOR REFLECTION

1. John writes, "God is light, and darkness is not in him, not at all" (1 John 1:5). In what specific ways does that news confront what you think about yourself? How does that news confront the way you live your life or the way you approach God?

2. When you speak about your sin, what kinds of things do you say to minimize your sin in the eyes of others (legalist)?

3. In the way you live your life, how do you minimize the importance of the law (libertine)?

4. John writes, "faithful he is and just, that he will forgive us our sins and cleanse us from all unrighteousness." Do you tend to downplay the faithful grace of God in the gospel, or the just righteousness of God in the gospel?

3
Growth

1 John 2:7–14

In the last chapter, we saw how John preaches the gospel to people with two extreme positions regarding God's law. On one side are the legalists, who insist that their salvation comes by their own ability to keep God's law. On the other side are the libertines, who argue that because they have been saved already, the law no longer applies to them. John refuses to give in to either side's errors. Instead, he argues that all of us need the gospel because we have fallen short of the perfect light of God's holiness but that our salvation through the cleansing blood of Jesus Christ leads us toward holiness, not away from it.

Now, John transitions to describing the growth that Christians ought to expect in our lives. Practically speaking, growth in discipleship leads us deeper and deeper into love. Love is the subject that comes up again and again through this letter. Of course, John isn't talking about some kind of fuzzy, flowery, sappy emotional love (the apostle is not a first-century hippie); he is describing a love that is far more substantial. John writes:

> ⁷Beloved, I am not writing a new commandment to you but an old commandment, which you have had from the beginning. The old commandment is the word that you have heard. ⁸On the other hand, I am

writing a new commandment to you, which is true in him and in you, for the darkness is passing away and the true light already is shining. (1 John 2:7–8)

The commandment John is talking about in these verses is the commandment to love. Right away, John refocuses our attention on love by addressing us as "beloved" and then immediately offering a paradox: the commandment to love is so old as to have been from the beginning, but it is also brand new. Later, in verses 9 to 11, John will speak explicitly about love by contrasting those who hate their brother and are in darkness (verse 9) with those who love their brother and abide in light (verse 10).

THE OLD COMMANDMENT

John begins this section on growing in love by reminding us that the commandment to love is quite old: "Beloved, I am not writing a new commandment to you but an old commandment, which you have had from the beginning. The old commandment is the word that you have heard" (1 John 2:7).

John is not exaggerating the age of this commandment. Even when Jesus declared that to love God and to love people were the two greatest commandments, he wasn't inventing anything new.[1] In fact, he was simply quoting two of the oldest commandments in the Old Testament law:

You shall not take vengeance or bear a grudge against the sons of your own people, but you shall love your neighbor as yourself: I am the LORD. (Leviticus 19:18)

[4]Hear, O Israel: The LORD our God, the LORD is one. [5]You shall love the LORD your God with all your heart and with all your soul and with all your might. (Deuteronomy 6:4–5)

Speaking about these two commandments, Jesus stated, "On these two commandments depend all the Law and the

Prophets" (Matthew 22:40). In other words, he is emphasizing that all the law (and the prophets, for that matter) are commandments about love.

John wants his readers to remember that they have had the commandment to love "from the beginning" and that the commandment to love is "the word that you have heard." If his readers were raised in Jewish homes, they would have grown up hearing, singing, and memorizing the law, so this commandment was the word they would have heard again and again and again. But even if some of his readers were Gentile converts to Christianity, John is reminding them that he had preached the commandment to love from the beginning.

HOW JESUS MADE THE OLD COMMANDMENT NEW

Then in verse 8, John suddenly seems to change his mind, now telling us that the commandment is a "new commandment." How can the commandment be ancient but yet also new? In fact, Jesus has made the old commandment new in at least three ways.[2]

First, Jesus put a new emphasis on love. As we read earlier, a major emphasis in the ministry of Jesus was to show how fulfilling the Old Testament law was essentially a matter of learning to love God and to love other people. Jesus refused to get bogged down and sidetracked by legalistic discussions on the specific kinds of activity that would be permissible on the sabbath or on the proper method of hand-washing, for example. Instead, he brought new clarity to the law by reframing the entire discussion away from technicalities and toward demonstrating love.

Second, Jesus gave us a new example of love. Jesus was not like the Pharisees who "tie up heavy burdens, hard to bear, and lay them on people's shoulders, [when] they themselves are not willing to move them with their finger" (Matthew 23:4). Instead, Jesus modeled love perfectly and insisted that anyone who would become his disciple follow the example that he set. Accordingly, on the night before Jesus died, he spoke with his disciples, saying, "A new commandment I give to you, that you love one another: just as I have loved you, you also are to love one another" (John 13:34).

Again, Jesus is telling his disciples nothing new, since the Old Testament had always commanded love. Even so, Jesus nevertheless insists that he is giving them a new commandment. Why? Because the commandment to love now carries with it the standard set by Jesus himself: "just as I have loved you, you also are to love one another." Jesus said this right after he had finished washing the feet of his disciples, a task reserved for the lowliest servant on hand. Jesus pointed to what he had done, and asked:

> 12Do you understand what I have done to you? 13You call me Teacher and Lord, and you are right, for so I am. 14If I then, your Lord and Teacher, have washed your feet, you also ought to wash one another's feet. 15*For I have given you an example*, that you also should do just as I have done to you. (John 13:12–15)

Here, Jesus does something extraordinary by washing his disciples' feet, and, even more incredible, in less than twenty-four hours he would go to the utmost length for his disciples by dying for them on the cross. If we want to know what love looks like, we need to look at Jesus for the perfect example.

Third, Jesus provides a new enabling to keep the commandment. Notice how John tells us this new commandment "is true in him and in you, for the darkness is passing away and the true light already is shining" (1 John 2:8). It is odd to speak of a commandment being true. For example, if a parent told a child to clean his room, the child would not argue with his parent by saying, "That's not true!" We don't usually speak of commandments as being true or false.

So what does John mean by this? John is speaking about the fulfillment of the commandment, not about the commandment itself. He is reminding us that we ourselves are incapable of keeping the law. As disciples of Jesus, we know legalism is a lie, but we also know God doesn't abolish the requirements of his law simply because we are incapable of keeping the law. Instead, he sent Jesus to fulfill the law on our behalf, in our place. The fulfillment of the commandment is true in him.

But John goes one step further, telling us that the fulfillment of the commandment is true *in us* as well. Our relationship to Jesus Christ through faith does not merely wipe our guilty slate clean so that we can have a second chance to try harder to please God—that would only plunge us right back into legalism.

In fact, the gospel does better than that. Through faith in the gospel of Jesus, God makes us righteous in Christ. Then, God gives us real spiritual growth by working in our lives by the power of the Holy Spirit. As we grow in the gospel, God actually changes us to be like Jesus so that, more and more, this commandment is true in us, just as it was true in Jesus himself.

THE LITMUS TEST OF GENUINE FAITH

Now, we need to be very clear: Jesus, and only Jesus, fulfilled the law completely through his perfect life, death, and resurrection. There is nothing more whatsoever that we need to do, or that we even could do, to bring Jesus' work to completion. We are saved completely by what Jesus has done and not at all by what we do. Salvation comes by faith alone in Christ alone as we trust Jesus to do for us what we could never do for ourselves.

But at the same time, saving faith is never alone. True, genuine, saving faith always produces growth. If we say that we have faith but our lives never reflect spiritual growth toward maturity, we need to question whether or not our faith is genuine. This isn't to say that we should spiral into

31

despair every time we falter in our faith by falling back into sin, because all believers will continue to sin in this life. John even told us, "If we say that we do not have sin, we deceive ourselves, and the truth is not in us" (1 John 1:8), so pretending that we do not continue to struggle with sin in our lives is not an option John leaves on the table.

So, instead of seeking perfection, John's point is simply that we should be able to identify genuine ways that God has begun to change our lives. Of course we must acknowledge that we will never be perfect on this side of eternity, but we should be able to see growth. Remember, the libertines who believed they could reject obedience to the law altogether were just as mistaken as the legalists who believed they could be saved through their own ability to keep the law.

On that subject, we come to 1 John 2:9–11. John's words here are hard, and they should give every sincere Christian pause:

> 9The one who says that he is in the light but hates his brother is in the darkness up to now. 10The one who loves his brother abides in the light and in him is not a stumbling block. 11But the one who hates his brother is in the darkness and walks in the darkness and does not know where he is going, for the darkness has blinded his eyes.

Love is the standard of the law. But, while we are not allowed to ignore it like the libertines, we should remember that we will fail at times to keep this law perfectly. Where we fall short, we need to return to the gospel, confessing our sins and believing that the blood of Jesus, our advocate, will cleanse us of all unrighteousness. Here again, we are called to walk the path of the gospel instead of falling into error on either side, whether the error of legalists or of libertines. John refuses to soften God's requirement that we love one another, but he also reminds us God does not save us based on our ability to keep his law.

Jesus alone can save us through his gospel, but the

salvation Jesus offers is not some Get Out of Hell Free card we put in safekeeping for the future, only to return to living our lives in the same ways that we always have. The gospel is bigger than that. As we continue to grow in the gospel, God continues to transform us away from walking in the darkness of hatred and toward abiding in the light of love. Faith alone saves, but because of the power of God's gospel, saving faith is never alone. Real, transforming, genuine faith in Christ will always lead to good works and substantive growth in our ability to love our brothers and sisters.

But if we continue to hate our brothers and sisters without any real transformation in our hearts, and if the gospel is making no inroads to change us, however slow that process might be, then the fact of the matter is we continue to walk in darkness, despite what we might say about being in the light.

THE BELOVED CHURCH

John summarizes all he has said to this point in a poem in 1 John 2:12–14:

> [12]I am writing to you, little children [*teknia*],
>> for your sins have been forgiven for his name's sake.
>
> [13]I am writing to you, fathers,
>> for you have come to know the one *who is* from
>> the beginning.
>
> I am writing to you, young men,
>> for you have overcome the evil *one*.
>
> [14]I wrote to you, little children [*paidia*],
>> for you have come to know the Father.
>
> I wrote to you, fathers,
>> for you have come to know the one *who is* from
>> the beginning.
>
> I wrote to you, young men,
>> for you are strong,
>> and the word of God abides abides in you,
>> and you have overcome the evil *one*.

In this poem, John writes with a simplicity that masks his profound insights into the gospel. To better understand what he is saying, it is important to recognize John is addressing not three classes but two, as John Calvin (1509–64) and others explain.[3] The two words John uses for "[little] children" in this passage do not refer to young people but rather to the entire church. Through this letter, John uses the same two terms to address the church as as a whole. He uses the word from verse 12 (*teknia*) in 1 John 2:1, 2:28, 3:7, 3:18, 4:4, and 5:21; and he uses the word from verse 13 (*paidia*) in 1 John 2:18.

In addition to addressing the church as a whole, John is addressing two classes specifically: the old ("fathers") and the young ("young men"). The Greek language uses gender in ways that English does not, so the masculine words for "young men" and "fathers" also would include females in that category. The terms are gender inclusive, and John is actually focusing on all the old in the church and the young in the church, in addition to focusing on everyone together when he speaks about the "children."

So what does John say to the children? He reaffirms the gospel: "your sins have been forgiven for his name's sake" (2:12) and "you have come to know the Father" (2:14). To John, these doctrines (in systematic theology, the doctrines of justification and of adoption, respectively) are more than abstract theory—they mark the core identity of every believer. Our sins are forgiven for the sake of Jesus' name. We have been adopted into the family of God so that God has become our Father. No wonder John opens this section by addressing the church as "beloved" (2:7), for that is what we are!

Then, John builds on this reality in his comments to the young. Not only does every believer know firsthand the precious realities of forgiveness and adoption; all young people have been made strong and have overcome the evil one, for the word of God now abides in them. Notice that Christians do not accomplish acts of strength to be saved; they are saved because Christ has accomplished all this on their behalf, so that what is true in Christ is true in them (2:8).

So, is John describing an aggressive, headstrong Christian who is always willing to pick a fight for Jesus? Hardly. If the word of God abides in these youths, then their lives are marked by love rather than aggression: "Whoever keeps his word, truly in this one the love of God has been perfected" (1 John 2:5). Following in the footsteps of Jesus, our strength is seen in the degree to which love directs our actions.

Finally, John further connects these gospel realities to lives marked by love in his simple comment to the old: "you have come to know the one who is from the beginning." Who is from the beginning? Jesus Christ is: "What was from the beginning...who was toward the Father and was manifested to us.... And our fellowship is with the Father and with his Son Jesus Christ" (1 John 1:1–4).

But consider what John means by knowing Jesus. Knowing Jesus means obeying his commandments, and his commandments are summarized in a law of love: "The one who says that 'I have come to know him' but is not keeping his commandments, he is a liar and the truth is not in him. Whoever keeps his word, truly in this one the love of God has been perfected" (1 John 2:4–5).

All we children of God—young and old—are beloved by the Father in Jesus Christ by faith through the Holy Spirit. Our sins are forgiven, and we have been adopted by the Father as sons. And all we children of God—young and old—are to walk in a manner marked not by sin and darkness but by love. This is the high privilege and calling of those who have come to know the love of God through the gospel of Jesus.

QUESTIONS FOR REFLECTION

1. If you had to sum up the central message of the Old Testament in one word, would you choose the word *love?* Why or why not?

2. Compare how Jesus carries forward the Old Testament's message of love with the way that Jesus makes that old commandment new. What does Jesus keep the same, and what does Jesus change in his connection with the Old Testament?

3. What does it mean when we say, "Faith alone saves, but saving faith is never alone"? How does this help clarify the middle road of the gospel between the errors of the legalists and the errors of the libertines?

4

Perseverance

1 John 2:15–27

Seeking real growth through the gospel is a grueling, lifelong marathon of learning to depend on Jesus instead of self—whether self-righteousness (on the legalist extreme) or selfish desire (on the libertine extreme). Discipleship is not a perfectly even, gradual ascent into heaven; it is an up-and-down journey from the top of glorious Mount Zion all the way down to the valley of the shadow of death and back again.

On top of that, disciples of Jesus must deal with the reality of external pressures, lies, and temptations that make the Christian life even more difficult. We have a great privilege to follow Christ in the company of other believers who are on the same journey, but make no mistake: not everyone in the world prays for our eventual success. In 1 John 2:15–27, John gives a sharp warning: don't let anyone or anything tempt you away from following Jesus.

THE WARNINGS ABOUT THE WORLD

The most obvious lies we face come from the world. Probably, when you think about temptation, your first thoughts go toward what the world constantly offers to you. In fact, there are other, more serious deceptions we will address in the next section of this chapter, but first, John alerts us to the dangers found in the world. He writes:

> [15]Do not love the world, nor the *things* in the world. If anyone loves the world, the love of the Father is not in him. [16]For everything in the world—the desire of the flesh and the desire of the eyes and the pride of life— is not from the Father but is from the world. [17]And the world is passing away, but the one who does the will of God abides forever. (1 John 2:15–17)

DO NOT LOVE THE WORLD

Notice specifically how John phrases his warning in verse 15: "Do not love the world, nor the things in the world." John does not speak right away about our behavior (what we do), but he instead asks us to identify what it is that we love. It is easy to tell what someone loves best by asking one simple question: What does this person choose? If we say that we love Jesus (and not the world), what really happens when the world offers us something that would require disobedience to Jesus? Do we choose Jesus, or do we choose the world and the things in the world?

Augustine, an African bishop who lived 354 to 430, preached a sermon to help identify what it is that we actually love. He asked:

> If someone asked you, "Which is better, money or wisdom, money or justice, or finally, money or God?" you wouldn't hesitate to answer: "wisdom, justice, God." You must hesitate as little when you're actually making a choice as when you're giving an answer. Which is better, justice or money? Of course, you all shout out "justice!" as if you were children in class competing to answer the question first. I know you all; I can hear what you're thinking: "justice is better." But then temptation comes along. It offers you some money from somewhere else. Now temptation is saying to you: "Look, here's some money you could have; if you do a bit of cheating the money is yours." But justice

will ask you, "What are you going to choose? Now's my chance to test your words."

When you were listening to my questions just before, you preferred justice to money. But now—both of them are in front of you! Money on this side; justice on that side. You close your eyes against justice, as if you are ashamed, and you stretch out your hand to take the money. What an ungrateful idiot! When I questioned you, you preferred justice to money. You've acted as a witness against yourself. Will God call another witness when you've convicted yourself? You prefer justice so far as praising it goes; but when it comes to choosing you prefer money.[1]

This is a difficult question, isn't it? We say we love Jesus, but do we? When push comes to shove, what do we choose? What or whom do we really love? We will return to this question in a moment.

DO NOT LOVE THE THINGS IN THE WORLD

In verse 16, John chooses his list of worldly temptations carefully: the desire of the flesh and the desire of the eyes and the pride of life. These are not simply the first three temptations he arbitrarily brainstormed while writing this letter, but they represent a complete set of temptations that summarize all the world offers to us.

Either the world appeals to our bodily needs (food, comfort, sex) or to what entices us visually (beauty, luxury, power) or to our "pride of life." This last phrase is a bit tricky to translate, but it's important. The Greek word for "life" here is *bios*. We get our word *biology* from this word, which refers to the study (*-ology*) of life (*bios*).

Some English versions translate this phrase as having to do with possessions or riches, and with reason, since we come across the same Greek word in 1 John 3:17: "But if anyone has the world's goods [*bios*] and sees his brother in need, yet closes his heart against him, how does God's love abide in him?" (ESV).[2] In this verse, we might translate the word *bios* as "livelihood" to give an English equivalent of how a word related to "life" functions as "riches."

To return to our current passage, then, this word could have something to do with materialism or consumerism and the pride that comes from having many possessions. But in fact, this word actually has a meaning even broader than simply the desire to acquire a lot of stuff. R. C. H. Lenski explains that this word refers to a broader pride that seeks to live completely independently from God:

> This pretense does not ask regarding the Father's will but acts as though it had the sovereign direction of its course of life.... The translations "the pride of life" (A.V.), "the vainglory of life" (R.V.) convey the wrong idea; John has in mind that hollow arrogance which presumes that it can decide and direct the course of life without God, determine what it will do, gain, achieve, enjoy.[3]

This "pride of life," then, refers not so much to the physical things that our bodies desire, or that our eyes lust after, but rather to an overall outlook in life. Instead of humbly depending on God and his gracious love toward us, a pride of life desires only independence from God. This attitude wants control above anything else. Even people who deliberately avoid accumulating too many things still struggle with the desire to retain complete control over their lives. The "pride of life" is the final frontier of rebellion in our hearts.

Also, we need to recognize that these worldly desires are not new. In these three temptations, John is echoing the description of the fall of Adam and Eve into sin in Genesis 3. Compare "the desire of the flesh and the desire of the eyes and pride of life" with the following:

> So when the woman saw that the tree was good for food [desire of the flesh], and that it was a delight to the eyes [desire of the eyes], and that the tree was to be desired to make one wise [pride of life], she took of its fruit and ate, and she also gave some to her husband who was with her, and he ate. (Genesis 3:6)

Ever since Adam and Eve sinned in the Garden of Eden, human beings have faced temptations that appeal to the desire of our flesh (what our bodies seem to demand), our eyes (when appearance outweighs wisdom), and our arrogant self–direction (what we deem beneficial apart from God). The world offers powerful temptations with deep roots, so what can we do to stand against them? How do we fight temptations through faith in the gospel of Jesus and in the power of the Holy Spirit?

In other words, how do we stop loving the world (and the things in the world) and start loving Jesus more and more?

THE EXPULSIVE POWER OF A NEW AFFECTION

Answering this question, the Scottish pastor Thomas Chalmers (1780–1847) preached a famous sermon on this passage called "The Expulsive Power of a New Affection." He argued that there are really only two ways to try to change what we love. The first is to expose the lies of this world, demonstrating how this world really cannot offer the happiness, peace, and love it promises:

> There are two ways in which a practical moralist may attempt to displace from the human heart its love of the world—either by a demonstration of the world's vanity, so as that the heart shall be prevailed upon simply to withdraw its regards from an object that is not worthy of it....[4]

All the world has to offer is vanity, a chasing after the wind. This first option for changing what we love, Chalmers explains, basically tries to show the foolishness of pursuing the world's vanities.

Certainly, exposing the lies of the world ought to be part of our message. It is important we understand that when the world tempts us, it is making promises of pleasure and beauty and satisfaction that it cannot keep. Along these lines, Lenski writes:

Does the siren voice of the world tickle your ears? Hear the word of truth: "The world is passing away!" The bank is breaking, it was never solvent—will you deposit in it? The foundation is tottering, it was never solid but only sham—will you build on it? The mountain is rumbling, quaking, it was never anything but volcanic, ready to blow off its head at any time—will you build your city there?[5]

Exposing the problem this way gets us moving in the right direction, but it just isn't enough. We must come to understand that we need something beyond this if we really want to turn our hearts away from the "siren voice of the world." Our hearts are vacuums that were created to worship something, so the solution isn't just to stop loving the world. God made us with the intention that we would latch powerfully in love to him. The entrance of sin in the world did not destroy our need to love and to worship something; it only directed our attention away from God onto something else.

So, Chalmers goes on in his sermon to explain that the better way to wean ourselves off of the love of this world is to learn how to love Someone better. Here is the second option Chalmers describes for conquering the temptations of worldliness:

...or, by setting forth another object, even God, as more worthy of its attachment, so as that the heart shall be prevailed upon not to resign an old affection, which shall have nothing to succeed it, but to exchange an old affection for a new one.[6]

Rather than trying to starve our hearts from the pleasures of loving the world, we need to learn by personal experience that the feast at Christ's table is far better than the pleasures of this world. When we genuinely desire Christ more than we desire what this world has to offer, avoiding sin becomes much easier. Then, we don't have to grit our teeth, summon all our self-control and resolve, and say no to the world. Instead, avoiding temptation is as easy as joyfully saying yes to Jesus.

At the end of the day, we will always end up doing whatever it is we value the most. Our hearts were created to gravitate toward something. If we have never developed a taste for Jesus, then the powerful affections of our heart will draw us inescapably toward the world. But if we continue to learn to love Jesus more and more, it becomes increasingly easier to choose him over any temptation the world offers us, whether of the flesh, sight, or life.

THE WARNINGS ABOUT THE CHURCH

While John spent three verses warning his flock about the dangers they face from the world, he now turns his attention over the next ten verses toward alerting us to the danger we face from within our own ranks in the church. He writes:

> [18]Children, it is the last hour, and just as you heard that antichrist is coming, also now many antichrists have come, from which we know that it is the last hour. [19]They went out from us, but they were not from us. For if they were from us, they would have remained with us. But *they went out* so that it might be manifested that each *one* is not from us. [20]And you have an anointing from the Holy *One*, and you all know *the truth*. [21]I did not write to you because you do not know the truth but because you know it and because every lie is not from the truth. [22]Who is the liar except the one who denies that Jesus is the Christ? This one is the antichrist, the one who denies the Father and the Son. [23]Everyone who denies the Son does not have the Father either; the one who confesses the Son has the Father also. [24]*As for* you, let what you heard from the beginning abide in you. If what you heard from the beginning abides in you, you will also abide in the Son and in the Father. [25]And this is the promise which he promised to us: eternal life.

> [26]I wrote these things to you concerning those leading you astray. [27]But *as for* you, the anointing which you

received from him abides in you, and you do not have a need that someone should teach you, but as his anointing teaches you concerning all things and is truth and is not a lie, also just as it taught you, abide in him. (1 John 2:18–27)

When John says that we are living in "the last hour" (verse 18), he is not so much talking about the specific timing of when Jesus might return but about the condition of the church. Specifically, "the last hour" refers to the danger of antichrist within the church.

When John writes about antichrist, it's important to recognize that he is not talking about a single, apocalyptic figure to come at the very last hours of the world (the Antichrist) but about many antichrists who lived even in the first century, and who continue to live among us to this day. These antichrists are not world leaders but simply apostates who have left the church—people who "went out from us" (verse 19). The antichrists are not the worldly people John described in 1 John 2:15–17; instead, the antichrists are people who have emerged from within the church.

These antichrists, however, have a telltale difference that John wants us to see: "They went out from us, *but they were not from us*. For if they were from us, they would have remained with us. But they went out *so that it might be manifested that each one is not from us*" (1 John 2:19). Yes, John explains, these antichrists were indeed with us for a time; but no, John assures, these antichrists were not from us, and we know that they were not from us because they did not remain with us.

What, then, is the difference? What makes the antichrists what they are, and what makes us what we are? John does not name greed, anger, pride, or even sexual sin. Instead, the difference is in their theology. The antichrists do not have merely bad theology, but abominable theology. John rails against their doctrine in 1 John 2:22–25:

> [22]Who is the liar except the one who denies that Jesus is the Christ? This one is the antichrist, the one who

44

denies the Father and the Son. [23]Everyone who denies the Son does not have the Father either; the one who confesses the Son has the Father also. [24]As for you, let what you heard from the beginning abide in you. If what you heard from the beginning abides in you, you will also abide in the Son and in the Father. [25]And this is the promise which he promised to us: eternal life.

Take careful note of the antichrists' theological error. They do not hold minor differences of opinion on issues like baptism, end times, proper church government, or even predestination. Much worse, the antichrists are those who try to get to the Father while rejecting the Son. They are "antichrists" because they deny the Christ.

This is not an honest intellectual mistake but serious spiritual rebellion, because the Father loves the Son. Reflect for a moment on all the places in the New Testament where we catch a glimpse of the Father's opinion of his Son. At Jesus' baptism, the voice of the Father boomed from heaven, declaring, "This is my beloved Son, with whom I am well pleased" (Matthew 3:17). When Peter, having seen Jesus transfigured on the mountain, imagined that he would honor Jesus by placing him side-by-side with Moses and Elijah, the Father rebuked Peter from heaven, insisting, "This is my Son, my Chosen One; listen to him!" (Luke 9:35). And after Jesus humbled himself all the way to the cross, he pleased his Father to the highest possible degree:

> Therefore God has highly exalted him and bestowed on him the name that is above every name, so that at the name of Jesus every knee should bow, in heaven and on earth and under the earth, and every tongue confess that Jesus Christ is Lord, to the glory of God the Father. (Philippians 2:9–11)

Did you catch that last phrase? When the Son is glorified by all of creation, the Father is also glorified. The Father loves the Son in such a way that his own glory is tied up in the glory of his Son, who pleases him very much.

Even more, we read in the New Testament that the Son is the official, perfect representation of his Father. Jesus Christ is the "image of the invisible God" (Colossians 1:15), and in him, "the whole fullness of deity dwells bodily" (Colossians 2:9). The eternal Son of God is "the radiance of the glory of God and the exact imprint of his nature" (Hebrews 1:3). So, when we look upon the Son, we are seeing the glory of the Father because of the fact that the Son is the perfect image and representation of the Father. Therefore, when we love, worship, adore, and obey the Son, we also love, worship, adore, and obey the Father. But if, on the other hand, we reject the Son, we also reject the Father.

All of this tells us that the Father takes our treatment of his Son personally. Christology (theology about Christ) is not an abstract mental exercise. Christology is intensely practical because Christology is intensely personal to God. If we honor the Son, we honor the Father; if we dishonor the Son, we dishonor the Father. This is no small matter—at stake is the full weight of the glory of God.

Nevertheless, antichrists dishonor the Son. The antichrists of John's day (and still in ours) did not dishonor the Son so much by rejecting him altogether but by redefining him and insisting that he was either not fully God or not fully human. They dishonored him by arguing that they did not need the salvation he provided through his shed blood on the cross, the plan for salvation the Father and the Son had agreed upon before the foundations of the world were laid. The Father so loved the world that he gave the world his Son to be crucified for the world! What, then, could be more offensive than to reject the Father's beloved sacrifice?

John treats this error seriously. Notice again the length of what John writes. He warns briefly against the pleasures of the world in 1 John 2:15–17, but he spends much more time warning against the antichrists in the church in 1 John 2:18–

27. Clearly, he is not as concerned with the fleshly, attractive, prideful temptations of the world as he is with the appalling theological rebellion that had already begun to creep up within the church.

Here is the point: Cleaning up your life from worldliness is not enough. Becoming a member of the church is not enough. Children, let no one deceive you: only the Son of God—who fully pleases and glorifies his Father—is enough. Perseverance in the midst of the world's temptations and through antichristology in the church requires returning again and again to the gospel of Jesus Christ, who is the Father's beloved Son. The cleansing blood of Jesus is precious in the sight of his Father, and so we dare not despise it or minimize its value.

THE ANOINTING OF THE HOLY ONE

How then should we react to John's warnings about the world and about the church? John considers—and rejects—two main possibilities that were actually offered in the first–century church:

1. Should we simply rely on our common sense, trusting our own intuition and discernment to navigate through life?

2. Or, should we instead seek higher knowledge held by elite Christians who know the secrets of fighting temptation that common Christians like us do not?

John rejects both of these suggestions because they reek of faith in human ability and human wisdom. If our common sense were sufficient for guiding us through worldliness and heresy, then why would John write anything at all to us in the first place? And if elite Christians had the secrets, wouldn't John be among them? Why wouldn't he just tell us the secrets so that all of us could know them?

Instead, John writes the following:

> [20]And you have an anointing from the Holy *One*, and you all know the truth. [21]I did not write to you because you do not know the truth but because you know it and because every lie is not from the truth.... [26]I wrote these things to you concerning those leading you astray. [27]But as for you, the anointing which you received from him abides in you, and you do not have a need that someone should teach you, but as his anointing teaches you concerning all things and is truth and is not a lie, also just as it taught you, abide in him. (1 John 2:20–21, 26–27)

So, what is this anointing? The word here is *chrisma*, and it is closely related to the Greek word *christos*, or Christ. In fact, Christ means "Anointed One." John is teaching us, then, that we share in the anointing of Jesus, the Anointed One.

John tells us this anointing comes from "the Holy One" (*tou hagiou*), a name that could possibly refer to Christ (e.g., Mark 1:24, John 6:69, Revelation 3:7), but that does not necessarily single out the Son from the other persons of the Trinity (e.g., Revelation 16:5). "The Holy One" is a term used throughout the Old Testament (especially the prophet Isaiah, who constantly speaks of the Holy One of Israel) to refer to the one true God. So, to help us identify whom John has in mind by "the Holy One," let's look more closely at what the Scriptures teach us about anointing.

In the Old Testament, anointing was used to consecrate people for their particular offices. Prophets (e.g., 1 Kings 19:16), priests (e.g., Exodus 28:41), and kings (e.g., 1 Samuel 10:1) were all anointed to begin their respective ministries. The reason that Jesus is called the Christ (the Anointed One) is that he is the true Prophet, Priest, and King—he holds the ultimate anointing for each of these roles.

But although Jesus is the Anointed One (the Christ), he is not the one who anoints—that role belongs to the Holy Spirit. This is true in the Old Testament, for example, when

David was anointed king of Israel in the midst of his brothers. There, we read, "the Spirit of the LORD rushed upon David from that day forward" (1 Samuel 16:13).

Moreover, the Scriptures specifically attribute the anointing of the Anointed One (the Christ) to the Holy Spirit:

> "The Spirit of the Lord is upon me, because he has anointed me to proclaim good news to the poor,"… And [Jesus] began to say to them, "Today this Scripture has been fulfilled in your hearing." (Luke 4:18, 21)

> …God anointed Jesus of Nazareth with the Holy Spirit and with power. (Acts 10:38)

The Holy One, by whom Christ was anointed, and by whom we are anointed, is the Holy Spirit. John is telling us we can fight the temptation of the world and the errors from antichrists in the church by the anointing we have received from the Holy Spirit.

John boldly declares that "you do not have a need that someone should teach you" and that "his anointing teaches you concerning all things" (1 John 2:27). He wants us to know that Truth himself abides within us, because we too have the Holy Spirit. By the anointing of the Holy Spirit, we can stand firm against error from outside and inside the church.

Note carefully, though, that John does not simply assure us that we have the Holy Spirit and then turn us loose. He explains, "I did not write because you do not know the truth but because you know it and because every lie is not from the truth" (1 John 2:21). So, he doesn't write to tell us something we do not know but to confirm what we already know by the anointing of the Holy Spirit.

This means John is not dismissing *all* teaching from within the context of the church, since John himself uses this entire letter to teach us about Christian discipleship. Instead, John is simply warning us we should not trust people who offer new, secret, or hidden teaching. Faithful teachers will lead us deeper into God's word with the aid of the Holy Spirit and not into brand new teachings of their own invention.

There is a mystery here, and this is the same mystery we experience each time we reread the same passages from the word of God, and each time we gather to hear the word of God read, proclaimed, sung, and visibly portrayed in baptism and the Lord's Supper. The goal of hearing and rehearing the word of God isn't really to learn new facts, although that does often happen. The goal is that God would cause his word to bear fruit in our hearts and lives by confirming the truth in us again by his Holy Spirit.

We know the truth because we have the truth in us. John wants us to be established, rooted, grounded, growing, and experienced in the truth. When we intimately know and love the truth, we will not stumble because of any lies, whether lies of the world or those from some within the church.

Then, if we remain in the truth, we will gain the promise he made to us—eternal life (1 John 2:25). To find out what John means by this, simply peek ahead to the definition of "eternal life" he gives at the end of this letter: "And we know that the Son of God has come and has given us understanding, so that we may know him who is true; and we are in him who is true, in his Son Jesus Christ. *He is the true God and eternal life*" (1 John 5:20 ESV). If we remain in the truth, we gain Jesus himself for all eternity.

The Holy Spirit anoints us to confirm the truth to us so that we can gain the exquisite joy of a personal, intimate relationship with Jesus Christ, who is true God and Eternal Life himself. In response, we trust, worship, adore, obey, and delight in Christ to the glory of God the Father. The Holy Spirit anoints us with Christ, and Christ, in turn, reveals the full glory of the Father to us.

The more we continue in our journey of learning to love God—Father, Son, and Holy Spirit—the more we find strength to choose God over the temptations we face in every area of our lives. This is how we experience growth in the gospel, and this is how we persevere, by the grace of God, all the way to the end.

QUESTIONS FOR REFLECTION

1. In what ways do you feel the lure of "the desire of the flesh and the desire of the eyes and the pride of life"? In particular, how does the temptation of "the pride of life" manifest itself for you?

2. Describe your strategies for overcoming temptation in your life. Do you mainly try to say no to sin, or are you seeking to learn to love Jesus more than you love sin?

3. If you woke up tomorrow morning to realize that overnight you had come to love Jesus more than you love sin, what would be the first thing you would notice as different in your life?

4. In your thoughts, your speech, your behavior, and your worship, do you take Christology as seriously as God the Father does? What would change if you did?

5. What role does godly, faithful teaching play in your life? Is your goal to hear something new, or is it to grow deeper in truth through the anointing of the Holy Spirit?

5
Hope

1 John 2:28–3:10

O ver the course of a lifetime of following Jesus, the Apostle John faced many painful discouragements. John was at the cross, watching when his master died (John 19:26–27, 35). Early in his ministry, John was imprisoned with Peter for preaching the gospel (Acts 4), and he had a difficult ministry that included pastoring his people through schisms (1 John 2:18–19) and in the face of rebellious members in the church (3 John 1:9–10).

When King Herod began to persecute the early church, he killed John's brother James (Acts 12:2). In fact, tradition holds that John outlived all the other apostles (his closest friends), after most of them (if not all) were martyred for their faith. John himself was not martyred, but he was banished to the island of Patmos "on account of the word of God and the testimony of Jesus" (Revelation 1:9). John had to live out his remaining days in lonely exile after everyone he loved best had died.

John was thoroughly acquainted with sorrow, adversity, and grief, and he faced constant threats because of the message of the gospel he faithfully preached. Still, John's writings (his Gospel, his three letters, and the book of Revelation) are filled with hope, joy, and peace. John, then, has something important to teach us about how to have hope in the midst of all the suffering we face in our lives.

In the previous chapter, we looked at John's warnings to persevere in the face of dangers from the world and from within the church, but Christianity isn't about learning how to grit our teeth or to keep a stiff upper lip. In other words, the point isn't merely to survive. Our heavenly Father wants something better for us than living every moment of our lives on the verge of collapsing under the pressure of discipleship. Remember, Jesus said his yoke is easy and his burden is light (Matthew 11:30). The gospel is a message of hope.

This doesn't mean at all that discipleship is easy or that Jesus will somehow help us to avoid pain and suffering—no, Jesus tells us plainly we must take up our own cross if we want to follow him (Matthew 16:24). The German pastor Dietrich Bonhoeffer (1906–45) summarized Jesus' statement bluntly, so there would be no misunderstanding: "When Christ calls a man, he bids him come and die."[1] These were not empty words, as Bonhoeffer was eventually martyred in a Nazi prison camp for his faith.

John does not fill us with false hope of perpetual prosperity and abundance, but he also does not morbidly sulk in doom and gloom. John is realistic about the reality of pain, but ultimately, he lives by hope that things will not always be as they are now.

John wants to encourage us in the knowledge that one day, Jesus will return to set all things right. On that day, there will be no more tears. On that day, there will be perfect, lasting justice. On that day, we will even become like Jesus, for we will see him just as he is in his unveiled glory. That is the hope to which John looks next. He writes:

> [2:28]And now, little children, abide in him, so that when he is manifested we may have complete confidence and not shrink in shame from him at his coming. [29]If you know that he is righteous, you know also that everyone practicing righteousness has been born of him.

³:¹See what kind of love the Father has given to us, that we might be called children of God, and we are! Because of this the world does not know us, for it did not know him. (1 John 2:28–3:1)

ABIDE IN HIM

John finds hope exclusively in Jesus Christ. After concluding a difficult section in this letter about perseverance, he immediately encourages us to remember the source of our hope by a simple, gentle command: "And now, little children, abide in him."

Abide is a word John uses many times in this letter. He has already used the word ten times before this point, and he will use the word another eleven times before the letter is done.[2] The word means to "remain" or to "continue," and John uses it in this letter to describe a broad range of circumstances, including many aspects of our relationship with God, God's relationship with us, and our relationship to others in the church:

- We abide in Christ (1 John 2:6, 24, 27, 28; 3:6; 4:13).
- We abide in the Father (1 John 2:24).
- God's seed abides in us (1 John 3:9).
- The anointing of the Holy Spirit abides in us (1 John 2:27).
- We abide in the light (1 John 2:10).
- The word of God abides in us (1 John 2:14, 24).
- Those who do the will of God will abide forever (1 John 2:17).
- The antichrists did not abide with us (1 John 2:19).
- Those who hate their brother abide in death (1 John 3:14) so that eternal life does not abide in them (1 John 3:15); nor does the love of God (1 John 3:17).
- God abides in us (1 John 3:24; 4:12, 13, 15, 16).
- We abide in God (1 John 3:24; 4:13, 15, 16).

In chapter 2, verse 28, specifically, John is urging us to continue on in Christ. Again, if anyone knows deep discouragement firsthand, John does; however, John also knows the secret of how to avoid wallowing in self-pity when we begin to assess the bleakness of our situation. He knows how to cling to hope, and he teaches us that secret here.

Pay attention to the reason John gives in verse 28 as to why we ought to "abide in him": "so that when he is manifested we may have complete confidence and not shrink in shame from him at his coming." John is teaching us to look far beyond the immediate pain of the moment by reminding us of our future hope, that Jesus will return. When Jesus returns, he will come to judge the living and the dead, and on that day, those who have remained in Christ will stand boldly before him with confidence. Tragically, those who have not remained in Christ will shrink from him in shame at his coming.

So what does it mean to abide in Christ? Abiding in Christ is one of John's favorite ways to talk about discipleship. We abide in Jesus when we continue and remain in him. From what we have studied so far, we know that abiding in Christ requires knowing truth, believing the gospel, growing in love, and persevering through dangers from the world and from within the church. But John gives us a new angle in verse 29: "If you know that he is righteous, you know also that everyone practicing righteousness has been born of him." Abiding in Christ also means practicing righteousness.

For now, set aside the question of what it means to practice righteousness—we will get back to that when we look at chapter 3, verse 7, where John uses the phrase again and clarifies his meaning. Instead, reflect for a moment on a profound truth John slipped into his writing, almost completely unnoticed: "everyone practicing righteousness has been born of him." Everyone who practices righteousness (and therefore, everyone who abides in Christ as his disciple) has been born of God.

One of the greatest privileges of following Jesus is the knowledge that we do not follow him as slaves would, cowering in fear of the day Jesus will return to judge us along with the rest of the world. Instead, we serve Jesus as God's own children and as Jesus' brothers and sisters. John pleads with us to abide in Jesus because there is genuine joy there, the joy of knowing God as our heavenly Father. In chapter 3, verse 1, John overflows with his own wonder and joy at the kindness that God has shown to us: "See what kind of love the Father has given to us, that we might be called children of God, and we are!" This is not a prank from heaven or a deception from hell but an overwhelmingly joyful reality: we are God's own children!

This is where John finds hope in the midst of pain. This truth is the hinge on which his entire outlook hangs because it means that, no matter what might happen to him, he can appeal directly to his Father in heaven. No matter how bad things get, his elder brother Jesus is returning for him. In this truth, we can do more than endure life—after all, we are royalty, the children of the Most High King. Our enemy might harass us along the way, but the day is coming when he will be banished forever into the lake of fire, and we will reign along with Christ for all eternity.

Before we move to the next verses, don't miss the last phrase in 1 John 3:1: "Because of this, the world does not know us, for it did not know him." John wants us to begin to think about why it is we face such dangers in the world and from antichrists within the church. We are children of God, but not everyone shares in that same status with us. This difference causes significant hostility and even outright persecution from those who do not abide in Christ. John will explore this subject more deeply in chapter 3, verses 11 to 24, but he briefly raises the issue here. Take note of it now, and we will pick it up again in the next chapter.

WE SHALL BE LIKE HIM

John does not pack his robust, practical theology more densely into any other two verses in 1 John than he does in chapter 3, verses 2 and 3:

57

²Beloved, now we are children of God, but it has not yet been manifested what we will be. We know that when he appears, we will be like him, for we will see him as he is. ³And everyone hoping in him purifies himself, just as he is pure.

In these two verses, John sets up a tension he will carry all the way through the end of this section in chapter 3, verse 10.

The tension arises from the first two phrases in verse 2. First, John says, "now we are children of God." John has already stated that we are God's children (3:1), but by stating that we are God's children *now*, John clarifies that God is not putting our inclusion into his family off to some uncertain day in the far-distant future. Instead, John is saying, Now we are God's children, and that status cannot be called into question for any who remain (abide) in Christ—that is, for those who practice righteousness (1 John 2:28–29).

But this raises all kinds of questions: What does John mean when he talks about practicing righteousness? How much righteousness do I need to practice to remain God's child? What happens if I fall into sin? At what point am I disqualified for failing to obey Jesus? These concerns can haunt us, especially as we peek ahead to 1 John 3:6: "Everyone abiding in him does not practice sin; every one practicing sin has not seen him, neither has he come to know him." Or consider 1 John 3:8: "The one practicing sin is from the devil, for from the beginning the devil has been sinning." Under this definition, does anyone qualify as a child of God?

John encourages us with hope in verse 2: "it has not yet been manifested what we will be." Even though we are the children of God now, we have not yet grown into the fullness of that status—what we will be has not yet been completely manifested. Today, we see a glimpse of the glory, but the total glory we will one day enjoy has not yet been manifested.

Clearly, John is not saying that we must be perfect to remain as God's children. John has already rejected the legalistic approach to the law, and he is not reintroducing it here. If we twist part of what John says to argue that we must be perfect in this life, we have to ignore the rest of what he says acknowledging our ongoing limitations. In the Christian life, there is a constant tension between the already and the not yet. Already we are children of God, and already we resemble him, just as children resemble their human fathers. But we have not yet been fully transformed into the image of Christ, who already bears perfect resemblance to his Father. What we will be has not yet been manifested.

The remaining phrase in verse 2 in many ways resolves this tension: "We know that when he appears, we will be like him, for we will see him as he is." The good work that God has already begun in us (*now* we are children of God) will be completed when our future reality finally appears—on the day of Christ Jesus, and not before.

But there is even more here. We have now seen when the already/not yet tension will be resolved (when Jesus returns), but notice how we will ultimately gain the full glory of our status as children of God: "when he appears, we will be like him, for we will see him as he is." Somehow, in some way, simply seeing our Lord Jesus Christ will transform us to be like him.

Paul hints at something similar in 2 Corinthians 3:18: "And we all, with unveiled face, beholding the glory of the Lord, are being transformed into the same image from one degree of glory to another." Beholding the glory of the God in the face of Jesus Christ (2 Corinthians 4:6) is the catalyst for transforming the not yet into the already. This process begins now in part, but when Jesus returns our transformation will be made complete.

So, what are we supposed to do until that day when Jesus returns? How should we live in the present, while we are waiting to see Jesus in all his glory? John gives the answer in verse 3: "And everyone hoping in him purifies himself, just as he is pure." Because we are already God's children, but not yet fully formed into the image of Christ, we move in that direction as the Holy Spirit purifies us more and more, every day—that is, as we seek to become more and more like Jesus by the grace of God. Theologians call this growth "sanctification."

But for now, little children, abide in him. Now we are children of God, and our Father in heaven intends for us to live in anticipation of the day when our future reality will appear: the day when we become like Christ by seeing him as he is.

PRACTICING SIN, PRACTICING RIGHTEOUSNESS

In 1 John 3:4–10, John makes a startling claim: if we have indeed been born of God, we are not able to practice sin. The logic is simple: if we practice sin in an ongoing, unchecked way, then by definition, we have not been born of God. Read carefully what John says here, because this passage is easily misunderstood:

> [4]Everyone practicing sin also practices lawlessness, for sin is lawlessness. [5]And you have come to know that he appeared in order that he might take away sins, and there is not sin in him. [6]Everyone abiding in him does not practice sin; every one practicing sin has not seen him, neither has he come to know him. [7]Little children, let no one deceive you: the one practicing righteousness is righteous, just as he is righteous. [8]The one practicing sin is from the devil, for from the beginning the devil has been sinning. Unto this *purpose* the Son of God was manifested, that he might destroy the works of the devil. [9]Everyone having been born of God does not practice sin, for his seed abides in him, and he is not able to practice sin, for he has been born of God. [10]In this is manifest *who are* the children of God and *who are* the children of the devil: everyone not practicing righteousness is not of God, nor the one not loving his brother.

At first glance, John's demands seem impossible and overwhelming. Is he really saying we are children of the devil unless we are able to abandon sin completely? If I keep on sinning every week, every day, or even every hour, is that proof that God's seed is not in me? Who could possibly meet such an expectation?

But John isn't demanding perfection, and God isn't either. Seriously. This is clear from the section we just looked at in 1 John 3:2–3, when he insisted that now we are children of God, even though what we will be has not yet been manifested. John knows and acknowledges two truths here: although we are already God's children, we are not yet fully formed in the image of Christ.

So, instead of demanding perfection, John is actually describing what it means to purify ourselves, as he talks about in verse 3. Compare these two verses:

And everyone hoping in him purifies himself, just as he is pure [*kathos ekeinos hagnos estin*]. (1 John 3:3)

...the one practicing righteousness is righteous, just as he is righteous [*kathos ekeinos dikaios estin*]. (1 John 3:7)

Finally we come to the meaning of "practicing righteousness": John is purposefully drawing a parallel here between purifying yourself (i.e., lifelong, growing, progressive sanctification) and practicing righteousness. Practicing righteousness does not mean practicing perfection. Instead, practicing righteousness means we commit to ongoing purification throughout our lives by continuing to repent from our sin and believe in the gospel, trusting in God to give us growth in righteousness by grace.

Of course we will sin. Of course we will stumble. In fact, John has already told us, "If we say that we do not have sin, we deceive ourselves, and the truth is not in us" (1 John 1:8). He expects that we will sin, and he warns that anyone who says they do not sin is a liar.

When John talks about the person who is practicing sin, he does not mean someone who falls short of perfection but someone who refuses to repent from their sin altogether and who neither receives nor grows in the righteousness of

Christ through faith in his gospel. The Son of God appeared to destroy the works of the devil, and so whoever does not turn from the works of the devil and flee to Christ has no commonality with the Son of God at all. That person makes a practice of sinning, and therefore of lawlessness, for sin is lawlessness.

Sadly, many people misunderstand this concept, so they imagine the gospel of Christianity goes something like this: we believe that Jesus lived a good life, so we try to live a good life just like he did. The problem with this view is we will inevitably experience despair when we begin to compare our own success in practicing righteousness to the success Jesus had.

But the gospel of Christianity in fact says something startlingly different: we believe Jesus came to destroy every last bit of sin, death, and the devil. Rather than looking to Jesus as a model and trying really hard to live the perfect life he lived, we instead confess our complete inability to practice righteousness on our own. Instead, we believe that God, being rich in mercy, planted his seed inside of us to change our hearts so that we can no longer embrace sin as we once did and to cause us to repent and to turn to Christ for salvation.

Now we have become the children of God, even though what we shall be has not yet appeared, but we know that when he appears we shall be like him because we shall see him as he is. All who thus hope in him will practice righteousness (as he is righteous) by purifying ourselves (as he is pure) by grace and through faith in the one who practiced perfection for us and on our behalf.

Therefore, little children, *abide in him*.

QUESTIONS FOR REFLECTION

1. Why do you think John places so much emphasis on abiding in God, and on having God abide in us? How does that change the way we approach God and the way

we think about our relationship with him?

2. What effect does it have to know you are God's child *now*? What would be different if maintaining your status as a child of God were still in question?

3. How can we gaze upon Jesus now, even before he fully appears? Are you taking advantage of those opportunities to do so?

4. What would it look like in your life to pursue purifying yourself and practicing righteousness in ways you are not currently?

6
Righteousness

1 John 3:11–24

I n 1 John 1:5, John writes, "And *this is the message that we have heard* from him and proclaim to you, that God is light, and darkness is not in him, not at all." Now, in 1 John 3:11, John uses nearly identical language: "For *this is the message that you have heard* from the beginning, that we should love one another." In 1 John 1:5, John's message describes the nature of God, but here in chapter 3, John's message is proclaiming the commandment of God to love one another.

This isn't the first time John has written about love in this letter. In 1 John 2:7–11, the apostle tells about God's commandment to love one another. There, John describes the practical implications of love by using the imagery of walking in light versus walking in darkness—imagery he carries over from what he had written in 1 John 1:5–7.

By using in 1 John 2:7–11 the same language of light and darkness he had used 1 John 1:5–7, John is demonstrating that love in our lives is a reflection of God himself. God commands us to love so that we can begin to reflect one aspect of God's nature. If God is light, and darkness is not in him, not at all (1 John 1:5), and if we have fellowship with one another by walking in the light as God is in the light (1 John 1:7), then our love for fellow believers functions as proof that we abide in God's light (1 John 2:10). If we do not love other believers, then we betray the fact that we still walk in darkness (1 John 2:9) and that the darkness has blinded our eyes so that we cannot even see our lack of love for fellow believers (1 John 2:11).

So now, John is approaching the subject of love from a different angle, but he is again explaining the commandment to love one another by using language that describes God's nature. This time, instead of using imagery of light, John describes love with language of purification and righteousness.

As we explored in the last chapter, John explained that those of us who are God's children now will continually purify ourselves even as we recognize that what we will be has not yet appeared and that Jesus must appear before we can be fully transformed into being like him. Then, in chapter 3, verses 4–10, John gave the definition of purifying ourselves: practicing righteousness. Jesus came to take away sin (1 John 3:5) and to destroy the works of the devil (1 John 3:8) so that we would no longer practice sin in an ongoing, unrepentant way but instead practice righteousness, as God is righteous. "Everyone practicing righteousness," John writes, "has been born of him" (1 John 2:29).

In 1 John 3:11, John extends his definition one step further: we purify ourselves and practice righteousness when we obey the message that we have heard from the beginning, "that we should love one another." Again, by obeying God's commandment to love, we reflect a critical aspect of God's nature. The righteousness of God is love. To practice righteousness is to love as God loves.

This link between righteousness and love shouldn't surprise us, since Jesus himself taught us that to love God and to love other people were the two greatest commandments, both of which summarize the entire Old Testament law (Matthew 22:34–40). Then, Paul wrote that "love is the fulfilling of the law" (Romans 13:10) and that "the whole law is fulfilled in one word: 'You shall love your neighbor as yourself'" (Galatians 5:14). Perfect righteousness—the perfect keeping of the whole law—happens when we love one another.

John is circling back around to the subject of love because he wants us to understand love's centrality within Christian discipleship. Love is not a nice additional piece we are free to embrace or reject. Rather, love is at the core of what it means to follow Jesus, because love is at the core of God's own identity. As John continues to instruct us in the mystery of Christian love, he has three main lessons in this passage to explain the connection between love and righteousness: (1) why righteousness attracts persecution; (2) what love looks like in practical terms; and (3) how love gives us confidence before God.

John will return yet again to the subject of love later in his letter, but this passage is pivotal for understanding all John has to teach us about it.

WHY RIGHTEOUSNESS ATTRACTS PERSECUTION

John weaves back and forth between the linked concepts of love and righteousness in 1 John 3:11–15:

> [11]For this is the message that you have heard from the beginning, that we should love one another, [12]not like Cain, *who* was of the evil one and murdered his brother. And for what cause did he murder him? Because his works were evil, but *those* works of his brother *were* righteous. [13]Do not marvel, brothers, if the world hates you. [14]We know that we have passed over from death into life, for we love the brothers. The one not loving abides in death. [15]Everyone hating his brother is a murderer, and you know that every murderer does not have eternal life abiding in him.

The first lesson John has for us is that practicing righteousness (i.e., loving one another) will attract persecution. Certainly, God's people knew about persecution before John wrote this letter. In fact, John points all the way back to the fourth chapter of Genesis, when Cain (the son of

Adam and Eve) killed his brother Abel. Only one generation removed from perfection in the Garden of Eden and already a man is murdering his own brother!

Why did Cain murder Abel? John gives two reasons. First, Cain was "of the evil one." This phrase in verse 12 (*ek tou ponerou*) is almost identical to the phrase from verse 10, "of God" (*ek tou theou*), which is an abbreviated version of the phrase used in verse 9, "born of God" (*ek tou theou gegennetai*). The imagery John is using here cuts a strict division between the only two spiritual families that exist in the world. Either you are born of God or you are born of the evil one.

So what does John mean when he says Cain was born of the evil one? Jesus himself opened up the significance of the phrase when he accused some of the Jews of being the offspring of the devil: "You are of your father the devil, and your will is to do your father's desires. He was a murderer from the beginning, and does not stand in the truth, because there is no truth in him. When he lies, he speaks out of his own character, for he is a liar and the father of lies" (John 8:44).

If the devil's two sins are to murder and to lie, then it is interesting to reread Genesis 4:8: "Cain spoke to Abel his brother. And when they were in the field, Cain rose up against his brother Abel and killed him." Cain's murder in this passage is clear, but Jesus' statement helps us to understand what Cain might have spoken to his brother: lies. Cain was deceiving his brother to lure him out away from their parents into the open field where he could murder Abel without anyone to witness his crime or to stop him. Cain was a liar and a murderer, just like his father the devil.

The second reason John gives as to why Cain would murder Abel is this: "Because his works were evil, but those works of his brother were righteous." Going back to the story in Genesis 4, we learn that the Lord "had regard for" (i.e., looked favorably on) Abel's sacrifice "of the firstborn of his flock and of their fat portions" (Genesis 4:4) but that the Lord had "no regard for" Cain's offering "of the fruit of the ground." We are not told whether the problem with Cain's offering was what he sacrificed (plants vs. animals) or how he sacrificed (his heart before God), but it doesn't really matter. Either way, God confronted Cain about his poor sacrifice to encourage him and to warn him: "If you do well, will you not be accepted? And if you do not do well, sin is crouching at your door. Its desire is for you, but you must rule over it" (Genesis 4:7).

Cain, however, did not listen to God. Instead of ruling over his sin, he embraced it and murdered his own brother. We do not know everything that was happening in Cain's heart from the original story in Genesis, but John's description here gives us clarifying insight. In 1 John 3, we get the sense that Abel's righteous works cast shame on Cain's evil works so that Cain felt provoked to murder his brother to remove Abel as a standard of comparison. Rather than repenting from his evil works and seeking to obey God as his brother Abel did, Cain instead opted to eliminate his competition.

Frighteningly, Cain was not unique to react to his brother Abel with an envious rage that led him to commit murder. John explains that Cain's behavior is the norm we should expect from all those born of the evil one, and not the exception: "Do not marvel, brothers, if the world hates you" (1 John 3:13). To this day, those whose works are evil hate those whose works are righteous. To put it bluntly, your righteous actions can provoke enough hatred for someone to persecute and even to murder you!

But even if we recognize that righteousness does attract persecution, that still doesn't explain why this would be the case. What is it about righteousness that provokes hatred from those whose works are evil?

John gives us an important clue to help us answer that question in verses 14 and 15: "We know that we have passed out of death into life, for we love the brothers. The one not loving abides in death. Everyone hating his brother is a murderer, and you know that every murderer does not have eternal life abiding in him." In these verses, John is teaching us two important principles for understanding our own lives as well as our relation to the world.

First, John completes the handoff between righteousness and love: righteousness looks like love. From here to the end of this section, John does not again mention the word *righteousness* but shifts directly into talking about love for fellow believers without missing a beat. The way John writes this whole passage makes it clear that righteousness and love are not two separate categories in his mind, but connected activities. To practice righteousness (the thing that John has been urging us to do since chapter 3, verse 4) means to love our fellow believers. To make sure that we don't gloss over this important link, we will describe love in the rest of this passage as "righteousness-love."

Second, John teaches us that righteousness-love is miraculous and supernatural. When we come to salvation through faith in the gospel of Jesus Christ, we actually pass "over from death into life." In turn, this supernatural life then creates in us a love for other Christians. Apart from this life, we cannot love the brothers and we abide (remain/continue) in death. So, anyone who still hates another Christian does not have eternal life and continues in the footsteps of Cain and of the evil one.

By explaining the supernatural nature of love, John is planting an idea he will bring to fruition in verses 19 to 24, which is that love offers a kind of assurance of our salvation. In fact, John tells us, even persecution offers its own kind of assurance. Here's the gist of what John is saying: When we experience persecution because our works are righteous, that persecution is a sign God has radically transformed our nature to be like his. And, if we begin to resemble God by practicing righteousness-love like God's righteousness-love, then that resemblance is evidence of the fact that we have passed from death to life, having been given new birth to become like him as God's own children.

But as we start to evaluate the strength of this evidence in our lives, two questions arise: (1) What actually constitutes true, genuine, supernatural righteousness-love? and (2) How much assurance can we really gain from righteousness-love in our lives? We'll look at both of those questions next.

WHAT RIGHTEOUSNESS-LOVE LOOKS LIKE IN PRACTICAL TERMS

If, as John tells us, righteousness-love is an important proof to assure us that we have, in fact, passed over from death to life, then it becomes of the highest importance for us to evaluate our lives. Is this righteousness-love present in our lives, or not? What kind of love are we looking for?

There are so many different definitions of love in the world, so we need to be crystal clear about what we are talking about. John, in fact, is very specific in 1 John 3:16–18:

> [16]In this we have come to know the love, that he laid down his life for us, and we ought to lay down our lives for the brothers. [17]But whoever has the livelihood of the world and sees his brother having need and closes his heart from him, how does the love of God abide in him? [18]Little children, let us not love in word or in tongue but in work and in truth.

Many English translations smooth out an important word in verse 16. For example, the ESV says, "By this we know love, that he laid down his life for us, and we ought to lay down our lives for the brothers." But literally, verse 16 reads, "In this we know *the* love." The word *the* doesn't make much sense in English, unless you change the verse up a little. The King James Version (KJV) adds the phrase "of God" to emphasize the distinction John is making: "Hereby perceive we the love of God."

The KJV's paraphrase of the verse gets at the nuance of the word *the* in Greek, which is functioning as though it were the word *this*: "By this we know *this* love." In other words, John is specifically limiting the word *love* to the kind of righteousness-love he has been talking about so far. Donald Burdick explains the word *the* here "serves to identify the specific love John has in mind—God's active, sacrificial love manifested at the cross."[1]

The point is we are not allowed to choose for ourselves the definition of this love. Instead, John tells us exactly what *this* righteousness-love looks like: laying down our lives for fellow believers. If we want to practice this righteousness-love, then we must sacrifice our own comforts, possessions, conveniences, and even our own lives for the good of brothers and sisters in Christ.

But John purposefully does not allow us to keep this righteousness-love at arm's length by thinking about it exclusively in terms of whether or not we would die for someone. Certainly, some of us may face the decision whether to die for someone else at some point in our lives, but John is more concerned about how we live on a day–to–day basis.

In very plain and practical terms, John simply asks whether we would give up our worldly goods to serve fellow believers when we see their needs. Do our hearts drive us in compassion to give as we are able, or not? And if we ultimately shut our hearts against our brothers and sisters in Christ, then how could we possibly claim to have God's love in us?

John closes this section of the passage with a plea: "Little children, let us not love in word or in tongue but in work and in truth" (1 John 3:18). Please, let's stop merely talking about love and actually live according to what we claim to believe. If we say we are followers of Jesus Christ, the one who voluntarily gave up all the riches of heaven so that we might inherit the kingdom, and who willingly died so that we might live, then we ought to live as he lived by sacrificially giving away the worldly goods we possess when we see fellow believers who need them.

If we do, then by this we know that this righteousness-love of God dwells in our hearts and that we have passed over from death to life.

HOW RIGHTEOUSNESS-LOVE OFFERS ASSURANCE

In 1 John 3:19–22, John wants us to know how this

righteousness-love offers us assurance of our salvation. He writes:

> [19]And in this we will know that we are of the truth and will persuade our hearts before him, [20]for whenever our heart condemns *us*, God *is* greater than our hearts, and *he* knows all things. [21]Beloved, if *our* heart does not condemn *us*, we have confidence before God, [22]and whatever we ask, we receive from him, because we keep his commandments and we do what *is* pleasing in his sight.

Verses 19 and 20 are notoriously difficult to interpret. One commentator charts out "at least ten different possible ways of understanding verses 19–20," but John Stott helpfully explains that this passage's "general sense is clear, but it is grammatically confused, and the variant readings betray the difficulty which even in the earliest days was found in interpreting them."[2] These verses are actually fairly straightforward, even if we will have to work a bit to get at why John uses the grammar he does. Let's break this passage down by answering the three most difficult exegetical questions.

First, when John writes, "And in this we will know that we are of the truth and will persuade our hearts before him," the immediate question we should answer is whether "in this" refers backward to the previous context or forward to what John writes in verse 20 and following. Put another way, what is it that John points to as the evidence that provides us assurance in the face of our condemning hearts? Is it to the genuine love in work and in truth that we display (verses 16–18), or is it to something that John describes after verse 19?

The best answer is that John is looking backward since he doesn't give anything that might be the "in this" after verse 19. In verse 20 and following, John only explains the process of gaining assurance, without pointing to anything that might provide evidence for our salvation "in this." So, "in this" most likely refers to the way Christians do not close their hearts to fellow believers who have needs but instead love one another in work and in truth (verses 16–18). That kind of practical, sacrificial love in our lives functions as proof we can use to reassure our hearts before God.

Second, what does *persuade* mean? "Persuade" is the basic, literal translation of the word in verse 19, but most Bible translations don't use it. Of the major Bible versions, only the Holman Christian Standard Bible translates the word as "convince," which is a synonym of *persuade*. Otherwise, the major Bible translations uniformly translate this word as "assure" (KJV, New American Standard Bible), "reassure" (ESV, New Revised Standard Version), or even "set our hearts at rest" (New International Version).

This means the vast majority of Bible scholars who worked on this difficult passage recognize John had a specific kind of persuasion in mind: persuading our hearts toward reassurance when our hearts condemn us (verse 20). Despite the grammatical confusion, the general sense of what John has to say here clearly points toward how we go about finding reassurance before God.

Third, what does John mean in verse 20 when he says, "God is greater than our heart, and he knows everything"? Pointing to Paul's statement "I am not aware of anything against myself, but I am not thereby acquitted. It is the Lord who judges me" (1 Corinthians 4:4), some (like John Calvin) believe that this phrase refers to God's strictness in judgment.[3] These interpreters understand John to be saying that God knows even more to condemn in us than our own hearts do.

The problem with this interpretation is that the whole context, as we have seen, has to do with the exact opposite idea: how we reassure our hearts before God when our hearts condemn us. So, it's better to understand this phrase as encouragement. Most likely, John is telling us to stop riding the endless roller coaster of our feelings and to stop basing our confidence on our own perceptions of spiritual growth. John wants to move us away from the perpetual navel–gazing introspection that only leads to despair by reminding us that we simply don't have God's eternal perspective on the work he is doing in our lives. God is giving us eternal life and creating genuine love for our brothers and sisters in Christ, but that work doesn't all happen overnight.

C. S. Lewis (1898–1963) has a fantastic passage on our inability to judge our own spiritual progress in his book *Mere Christianity*:

> Christian Miss Bates may have an unkinder tongue than unbelieving Dick Firkin. That, by itself, does not tell us whether Christianity works. The question is what Miss Bates's tongue would be like if she were not a Christian and what Dick's would be like if he became one. What you have a right to ask is whether that management, if allowed to take over, improves the concern....
>
> We must, therefore, not be surprised if we find among the Christians some people who are still nasty. There is even, when you come to think it over, a reason why nasty people might be expected to turn to Christ in greater numbers than nice ones. That was what people objected to about Christ during His life on earth: He seemed to attract "such awful people."[4]

The question isn't, Am I perfect? Instead, the question John is teaching us to ask is, Is God doing a miraculous work in me by giving me more genuine love for fellow believers than I used to have? Yes, we need to look for the evidence of righteousness-love in our lives, but we should not go overboard by being too harshly critical of our inevitable failures. God is greater than our hearts, and he knows everything about where we began, where we are in our progress, and where he is taking us over the course of eternity.

At the end of the day, John wants us to rivet our attention on the kindness and love God demonstrates toward us. When we try to find eternal peace and security by looking at ourselves, we will waver in doubt as we find the failures that remain in our lives. But when we seek assurance for our salvation by taking our eyes off of ourselves and looking back at the character of God, who is greater than our own trembling hearts, our hearts can no longer condemn us and "we have confidence before God."

For this reason, John Calvin's perspective on this passage is extremely important, even though, as I mentioned earlier, I would quibble with his interpretation that the phrase "God is greater than our heart" refers to God's strictness in judgment. Calvin writes this warning about the assurance "if our heart does not condemn us, we have confidence before God" in verse 21:

> Here, however, arises a greater difficulty, which seems to leave no confidence in the whole world; for who can be found whose heart reproves him in nothing? To this I answer, that the godly are thus reproved, that they may at the same time be absolved. For it is indeed necessary that they should be seriously troubled inwardly for their sins, that terror may lead them to humility and to a hatred of themselves; but they presently flee to the sacrifice of Christ, where they have sure peace.[5]

We must find our ultimate confidence in eternal life in the promises of Jesus and not in anything within ourselves. Only in the sacrifice of Jesus do we have real, sure, lasting peace before God, and only through the sacrifice of Jesus do we receive answers to our prayers. When John writes in verse 22 that "whatever we ask, we receive from him, because we keep his commandments and do what is pleasing in his sight," he is not saying that our obedience obligates God. John Stott's line is helpful here: "Obedience is the indispensable condition, not the meritorious cause, of answered prayer."[6]

In fact, after John speaks of obedience in verse 22, he quickly clarifies that he is speaking of faith in the gospel of Jesus Christ:

> [23]And this is his commandment, that we believe in the name of his Son Jesus Christ and *that* we love one

another, just as he gave us *the* commandment. [24]And the one keeping his commandments abides in him, and he in him, and in this we know that he abides in us, by the Spirit whom he gave to us. (1 John 3:23–24)

True confidence, genuine assurance, and this righteousness-love flow only from the eternal life God gives to those who believe in the name of his Son Jesus Christ by his abiding Spirit. Recognizing spiritual fruit in our lives can be helpful, but we should not depend on that evidence more than we depend, by faith, on the finished work of Jesus Christ, because we are incapable of evaluating our own progress objectively.

Beloved, instead of incessant self-evaluation, let us believe the gospel and love one another, just as he has commanded us.

QUESTIONS FOR REFLECTION

1. Do you think it is accurate for John to link love and righteousness as he does in this chapter? How does it change the ways you think about righteousness and love if they are connected as John describes?

2. What worldly goods are you giving up right now for the sake of fellow believers?

3. Do you wrestle with assurance of your salvation? How should John's message in this section about persecution, persuading our hearts, and confidence change your perspective?

7
Discernment

1 John 4:1–6

O nce upon a time, there wasn't much confusion about what you were supposed to believe. You could always depend on the king or the priests or the prophets to go out of their way to ensure that you knew precisely what to believe on all the important issues. Certainly, some people had differing opinions, but their voices rarely carried very far into the public square—and if they did, those voices were generally not allowed to continue speaking much longer.

Of course, the kings, priests, and prophets might have been mistaken, and they might have even known they were not speaking the truth. That, however, was beside the point. The point was that they, and they alone, had the power to speak, so they alone had the ability to influence their respective listeners.

But then democracy happened. Common people began to speak out their respective opinions, and they were aided by new technologies that allowed their voices to carry increasingly far at an increasingly quick pace: the printing press, the telegraph, the telephone, the radio, the television, the computer, and now the internet. Suddenly, we live in a world where anyone can announce his opinion to the entire world about any issue, in any place, at any time, and he can do it right from the smartphone he carries in his pocket.

Chris Anderson's 2006 book *The Long Tail* tells the story of how technology fundamentally reshaped American culture and American media.[1] Even in the twentieth century, he writes, only those with a great deal of power, wealth, or influence had the technological resources to speak in the public square. By the twenty-first century, however, everything had changed. Three major changes made it possible for anyone to speak up and be heard.

First, the means of production were democratized with cheap hardware (computers, microphones, cameras, etc.) and powerful software. With these inexpensive tools, anyone can self-publish a book, record an album, or produce a video. Second, the means of distribution were democratized with internet superstores like Amazon, iTunes, and Netflix so that even the most unknown writer, musician, or filmmaker can get her creation into the marketplace and sell to anyone, anywhere. Third, advanced filters like Google's search engine or suggestive selling algorithms ("People who bought this book also bought…") connect buyers with exactly the kind of content they are looking for, regardless of the seller's geographic distance or obscurity.

The net result is that we live in world that incentivizes producing, distributing, and discovering hyper-specific niche media in every area of our lives, from commerce to entertainment to theology. We are bombarded with an unprecedented number of voices pushing us to think and act and believe in an unprecedented number of directions. With the click of your mouse or a swipe on your mobile device, you can access any conceivable kind of political commentary, sales pitch, theological treatise, terrorist propaganda, cooking recipe, pornography, encyclopedia article, hate speech, world literary classic, cat video, or indie music—and you can access all of it in a single afternoon.

We are inundated with influencers.

Test the Spirits

Because of this, John's plea is extraordinarily relevant today:

> Beloved, do not believe every spirit, but test the spirits *to see* whether *it* is from God, for many false prophets have gone out into the world. (1 John 4:1)

Even in John's day there were many false prophets in the world, despite the fact that none of them had the ability to publish a blog on the internet or to upload a video to YouTube. Still, John is not primarily concerned with the conspiracy theorist or the edgy youth but rather with a specific distortion of the truth that he will warn us about in 1 John 4:2–3.

Before we rush on to those verses, however, we twenty-first-century Americans desperately need to give our full attention to verse 1 by itself. Why? Because we rarely even try to test the spirits!

Certainly, we avoid crossing certain intellectual and philosophical lines. Liberals reject what they hear from conservatives, and conservatives refuse to listen to liberals; people who hold any religious beliefs (or who reject religion altogether) tend to become offended when their views are treated with contempt; and the list goes on and on. There is a reason Amazon has invested unimaginable amounts of money into suggesting the same kind of books to you as what you have already purchased: they wouldn't make as much money if they suggested books written from other perspectives, even if those books would balance out what you had already been reading!

Still, we hardly ever think about the vast majority of the messages that assail us every day. We completely miss the underlying consumerism conveyed in the commercials we find so funny. We have lost the ability to recognize that our favorite sitcoms are actually portraying a very particular, unbiblical worldview in regard to family, faith, sex, power, and money—and that they are portraying that worldview as

81

absolutely normal. We are numb to how deeply we are shaped by the songs we sing along with on the radio.

John is warning us to recognize that no message is ever value-neutral. Every message arises from some kind of spirit, and every voice is a kind of prophet for one spirit or another. Many false prophets have gone out into the world, and so John warns us to test the spirits carefully to see whether the messages we hear are from God or not. Before John teaches us how to exercise discernment and differentiate between the various spirits, he first alerts us here in verse 1 to the reality of false spirits and false prophets.

Do you ever evaluate the various voices you listen to? What is the message of the music, podcasts, or the talk radio programs that you listen to? What are your books and blog articles arguing? What kinds of discussions are you engaging with on social media? What exactly are all of these voices teaching you?

Are you prioritizing time for listening to the messages that are from God? Are you diligent to study the Bible? Do you listen carefully to the sermons your pastor preaches? When you hear the word of God, are you praying that God would teach you the truth of Jesus by his Holy Spirit?

THE DOCTRINE OF THE INCARNATION

Once we recognize the sheer number of messages we hear every day, John begins to teach us how to discern the difference between truth and error in them. In particular, John teaches us the specific truth he wants us to embrace and the specific error he wants us to avoid:

> ²In this you know the Spirit of God: every spirit that confesses Jesus Christ having come in flesh is from God, ³and every spirit that does not confess the Jesus is not from God, and this is the *spirit* of the antichrist, which you have heard is coming, and now is in the world already. (1 John 4:2–3)

82

At stake are three major issues. First, John is concerned about the doctrine of the incarnation, the idea that the Son of God took upon himself the fullness of human nature: Jesus Christ has come in the flesh.

There were two major heresies in John's day that denied some aspect of Jesus' incarnation. One, called docetism, held that Jesus only *seemed* to be human (the name of this heresy comes from the Greek word for "seem," *dokeo*) but that, in fact, he was not. The other, called adoptionism, held that the Divine Christ descended on the human Jesus from the point of Jesus' baptism and remained, departing the human Jesus just before the cross so that only the human Jesus, and not the Divine Christ, ever actually suffered. Both of these heresies stem from the belief that spirit is good and that physical matter is bad and that therefore God's Divine Spirit would never willingly unite himself to human matter or to human suffering.

In 1 John 2:18–27, John had written against those who question the full divinity of Jesus (i.e., his status as the only begotten Son of the Father), but here, John turns his attention to those who question the humanity of Jesus—his "having come in flesh"—since the incarnation is the foundation on which the entire Christian gospel rests. Quite simply, Jesus would not have been in a position to redeem and restore humanity if he had not been fully human himself.

The early church father Gregory of Nazianzus (330–90) put it this way: "For that which He has not assumed He has not healed; but that which is united to His Godhead is also saved."[2] In other words, Jesus was only able to save the aspects of human nature he himself took on through the incarnation. If he did not have a real human body or a real human mind or a real human will, then he could not have redeemed those aspects of humanity.

Also, the doctrine of the incarnation does not change the fact that Jesus was fully God. Notice the last part of Gregory's statement: "that which is united to His Godhead is also saved."

The glory of the incarnation is that Jesus was fully human and fully God. He did not lose his divinity, and he did not become some kind of hybrid between the two natures, half–human and half–God, but he took on every aspect of human nature while retaining every aspect of the divine nature at the same time.

If you find yourself confused about how this could be, you aren't alone. The early Christian church wrestled for centuries with this question, searching the Scriptures (including the passages we have been looking at in 1 John) and debating back and forth, trying to understand what exactly God had revealed about the human and divine natures of Jesus. At the Council of Chalcedon in 451, the representatives settled on a definition that is considered the standard of orthodoxy to this day, even if we still struggle to wrap our minds around all of its implications. Here is the full text of the definition:

> Following the holy Fathers we teach with one voice that the Son [of God] and our Lord Jesus Christ is to be confessed as one and the same [Person], that he is perfect in Godhead and perfect in manhood, very God and very man, of a reasonable soul and [human] body consisting, consubstantial with the Father as touching his Godhead, and consubstantial with us as touching his manhood; made in all things like unto us, sin only excepted; begotten of his Father before the worlds according to his Godhead; but in these last days for us men and for our salvation born [into the world] of the Virgin Mary, the Mother of God according to his manhood. This one and the same Jesus Christ, the only-begotten Son [of God] must be confessed to be in two natures, unconfusedly, immutably, indivisibly, inseparably [united], and that without the distinction of natures being taken away by such union, but rather the peculiar property of each nature being preserved and being united in one Person and subsistence, not separated or divided into two persons, but one and the same Son and only-begotten, God the Word, our Lord Jesus Christ, as the Prophets of old time have

spoken concerning him, and as the Lord Jesus Christ hath taught us, and as the Creed of the Fathers hath delivered to us.[3]

This definition makes it clear that Jesus was fully human and fully God and protects us from three dangerous errors. First, it is a mistake to think that Jesus' two natures were not fully united, as though his divinity and his humanity were divided like oil and water. So, Chalcedon made clear that Jesus held both natures without division and without separation.

Second, it is a mistake to think that Jesus' two natures combined to form an entirely new nature—no longer really human, and no longer really divine, but some kind of a third substance that is altogether different from the other two natures. So, Chalcedon insisted that Jesus held both natures without confusion and without change, "without the distinction of natures being taken away by such union" into a single person. Jesus' humanity is fully human, and his divinity is fully God, even though both natures are united into one person.

Third, it is a mistake to imagine that the human Jesus was a different person from the divine Son of God, as though Jesus had two personalities. So, Chalcedon clarified the "peculiar property of each nature being preserved and being united in one Person and subsistence, not separated or divided into two persons."

This definition is very clear, but there is a tension and mystery in this truth that our limited human minds really cannot fully resolve. How could Jesus be completely human and yet completely God? How could those two natures exist completely unified in one person, without any kind of confusion, change, division, separation, or annulment of any aspect? We are not called, however, to understand Jesus completely, since he is so much greater than we are. Instead, we are called only to believe the truth, to stand in awe of Jesus, and to worship him.

So, any spirit—and any prophet—that rejects, distorts, or mocks the doctrine of the incarnation is not from God but is the spirit of the antichrist. The incarnation is not a debatable point that Christians are free to believe or to reject. Apart from the incarnation, there is simply no hope of salvation.

CONFESSING THE INCARNATE CHRIST

The second issue at stake in 1 John 4:2–3 is that John has more in mind than just getting us to rubber-stamp the doctrine of the incarnation. This isn't something we assent to with our heads just to check off a prerequisite for entering the kingdom. Listen to Donald Burdick, who argues that confessing Jesus is something much deeper than a mere mental exercise:

> The KJV, NASB, and NIV all translate this confession as follows: "that Jesus Christ has come in the flesh." The weakness of this rendering is that the Greek text does not have the word *hoti* "that," and it is doubtful that it should be supplied in the English translation. Actually, to supply the word *hoti* is not an incidental matter, for it alters the very nature of the confession. With *hoti* the confession is propositional in nature. It is a declaration *about* what Jesus Christ did; without *hoti* the text contains a confession of Jesus as a person rather than a confession of a proposition about the Person. Brooke puts it aptly when he declares, "It is a confession not of the fact of the incarnation, but of the Incarnate Christ."[4]

So, rather than translating "every spirit that confesses that Jesus has come in the flesh," we need to read verse 2 this way: "In this you know the Spirit of God: every spirit that confesses Jesus Christ *who* came in the flesh is from God." Very literally, the phrase is "Jesus Christ having-come-in-flesh," so the entire phrase "having-come-in-flesh" functions as a single descriptive statement to clarify the specific Jesus Christ we are talking about. This is not a confession about facts we believe (the facts are assumed) but a confession of our faith in the person who came in flesh.

As we talked about in the first chapter, truth is a person. We do not believe in the incarnation as a theory, but our confidence is in the person of Jesus Christ who came in flesh, the God–man who healed us by uniting the fullness of our human nature to the fullness of his Godhead in the incarnation.

CONFESSING THIS HAVING-COME-IN-FLESH JESUS

Third, John goes one step further to insist upon the reality of Jesus Christ having-come-in-flesh. Donald Burdick is helpful once again concerning the clause "every spirit that does not confess Jesus [*ton Iesoun*, or "the Jesus"] is not from God" in verse 3: "John insists that it is 'this Jesus' who must be confessed— the Jesus of verse 2 who came in flesh (*en sarki eleluthota*)."[5]

Just as John had used the word *the* in 1 John 3:16 to emphasize this righteousness-love, so now he uses the word *the* to speak of *this* Jesus. This Jesus is the one whom the Spirit of God will confess, and this Jesus is the one we must confess. This Jesus is the Redeemer God who came to save his people by becoming one of them—by having-come-in-flesh!—and this Jesus is the Lion of Judah, the Lamb who was slain at the cross for our sins but raised up in victory over sin, death, and the devil at the resurrection. This Jesus is worthy of all worship, praise, adoration, glory, and honor. And any person who denies this Jesus (even by suggesting to you another jesus) is an antichrist, prophesying the message of a devil who wants to drag you to hell by any lie necessary.

Beloved, do not believe every spirit, but test the spirits to see whether they are from God, for many false prophets have gone out into the world, denying this Jesus who came in flesh.

THE DISCERNMENT OF THE SAINTS

So, if we are talking about evil spirits we cannot see but who have recruited prophets who are skilled in lying, what chance do we reasonably have of standing our ground? After all, our own faith isn't based on watertight logic, self–evident truths, or "lofty speech or wisdom" (1 Corinthians 2:1), but instead the good news of Jesus comes to us "in weakness and in fear and much trembling" (1 Corinthians 2:3). Should we be concerned about our ability to discern the difference between, on the one hand, the foolishness of men, which is the wisdom of God, and on the other hand, the folly of false prophets who lure us down the road to hell?

Yes and no.

Certainly, John means for us to have some kind of healthy concern about being led astray. If not, then he would not be exhorting us to "test the spirits" and warning us about all the false, antichrist prophets who are now in the world. We need to start paying attention to the messages we hear every day, in every corner of our lives.

But on the other hand, John isn't worried in the least. In fact, he doesn't continue on piling up warning on top of warning in the next few verses. Instead, he spends 1 John 4:4–6 explaining why there is no reason to become overly concerned:

> [4]You are from God, little children, and you have overcome them, for greater is the one in you than the one in the world. [5]They are from the world, for this *reason* they speak from the world, and the world listens to them. [6]We are from God. The one knowing God listens to us. The one who is not from God does not listen to us. From this we know the Spirit of truth and the spirit of error.

We have already overcome these false prophets! We are not marching into a hopeless battle, but we are instead marching in a victory parade. Of course, we ourselves contributed nothing to this victory. We have overcome the world exclusively because the one who is in us is greater than the spirit of error who is in the world.

More than that, God has graciously given us supernatural ability to overcome the lies of the evil one through discernment between truth and error. I love what John Stott writes about this:

This "overcoming" is not so much moral (as in ii. 13, 14, where the same word occurs) as intellectual. The false teachers have not succeeded in deceiving you. Not only have you tested them and found them wanting, but you have conquered them. You have not succumbed to their blandishments or believed their lies.[6]

The fact of the matter is that God has given us ears to hear his voice—that is, the voice of his Spirit of truth through his faithful prophets. John is not being arrogant when he says, "We are from God. The one knowing God listens to us. The one who is not from God does not listen to us. From this we know the Spirit of truth and the spirit of error" (1 John 4:6). Rather, he is speaking as an apostle who has been charged with delivering God's word faithfully, as though God himself were uttering the words. Whoever listens to the apostolic witness that has been preserved for us in the Scriptures, then, is from God.

And so this passage imparts to us a comfort and an admonition. We should be comforted by the fact that he who is in us is greater than he who is in the world. We have the Holy Spirit (Truth himself!) reigning in our hearts and anointing us with his knowledge, and we should be comforted by the fact that God will not ultimately allow his children to be deceived.

But we also should be warned against the deceitfulness of the world. There are many spirits in the world, and those spirits have recruited many antichrist prophets to spread their malicious propaganda. Do not be deceived—these forces are cunning and brutal. They will destroy you to whatever extent they are able.

So test the spirits, and do so by clinging to Christ by his Holy Spirit. This Jesus who came in flesh has overcome the world.

QUESTIONS FOR REFLECTION

1. What voices are you listening to regularly in your life? If you began to see those voices as prophets, then how would you characterize the spirits they are prophesying for?

2. How does understanding the incarnation of Jesus change the way we interact with all of creation, including how we think about and interact with ourselves?

3. What are you really depending on to defeat the lies of Satan? Your own wisdom and strength, or the wisdom and strength of the Spirit of truth? What would be different if you were depending fully on the Spirit of truth?

8
Love

1 John 4:7–21

So far in 1 John, the apostle has spoken at length on four main subjects:

1. The perfect righteousness of the God-who-is-light, in whom there is no darkness whatsoever (1 John 1:5). This righteousness is characterized by love (1 John 3:10).

2. Our sin (1 John 1:6, 8, 10), which has infinitely alienated us from the God-who-is-light. Additionally, John warns us not to fall back into sin (1 John 3:4–10), whether through the temptation of the world (1 John 2:15–17) or the lies of antichrists (1 John 2:18–27, 4:1–6).

3. Our salvation, which was purchased by the blood of Jesus Christ (1 John 1:7), who is the eternal Son of God (1 John 2:22–23), yet who became human (1 John 4:2–3) and submitted to death to propitiate (i.e., to appease) the Father's wrath against our sinfulness (1 John 2:2). Through Christ, we have already become God's children, even though the fullness of our glory has not yet appeared (1 John 2:28–3:3).

4. Our love for one another (the brothers), which is the litmus test for the genuineness of our faith and our salvation (1 John 2:9–11, 3:11–24).

Many commentators describe John's writing in this letter as a spiral, in contrast to the straight line of logic the Apostle Paul typically uses in his writing. Paul writes by developing an argument verse by verse, chapter by chapter, always building on what he has already written and rarely going back to pick up topics again that he has already covered in a particular letter. John, on the other hand, circles back again and again to these four major emphases. John never repeats what he has already said, but he is always spiraling in from one theme to another, then to another, then the next, and then back again to the first. Bit by bit, he gets closer and closer to the core of his message, until he arrives at the center of his message at the very end of this letter. Not a word is wasted, but John never gives his exhaustive message on any subject in a single shot.

In 1 John 4:7–21, John ties all of these themes together explicitly for the first time. He explains the link between the four themes in this way: since (1) God is love, and since (2) we are sinners who have been (3) saved by God's gracious love, (4) we ought to love one another in the same way God has loved us. John writes:

> ⁷Beloved, let us love one another, for the love is from God, and everyone who loves has been born of God and knows God. ⁸The one who does not love does not know God, for God is love. ⁹In this the love of God is manifested among us, for God has sent his only begotten Son into the world in order that we might live through him. ¹⁰In this is the love, not that we have loved God, but that he has loved us and sent his Son *to be the* propitiation concerning our sins. ¹¹Beloved, if in this way God loved us, we also ought to love one another. ¹²No one at any time has beheld God. If we love one another, God abides in us abides and his love is perfected in us. (1 John 4:7–12)

Here, John gets to the core of his message about Christian love. As we looked at in our study of 1 John 3:11–24 in chapter

6, John grounds God's commandment to love one another in the character of God, "for God is love." In this passage, John calls our attention to three characteristics of God's love that prove how necessary it is that we should love one another, just as God has loved us.

WE ALSO OUGHT TO LOVE ONE ANOTHER

First, John reminds us that God is the source of love: "Beloved, let us love one another, for the love is from God, and everyone who loves has been born of God and knows God" (1 John 4:7). All love comes from God, John writes, so anyone who loves does so because of their relationship to God ("everyone who loves has been born of God") and their intimate, personal knowledge of God ("and knows God"). God is like a master artisan who teaches his signature craft only to his children. We can reasonably infer that someone is a child of God if we see that person loving others in the same way that God loves us.

Let's be very clear about the implications of what John is saying: only Christians are capable of this kind of love. John is explicit on this point; however, it is important to recognize that John is not saying that non-Christians are incapable of loving their parents, their siblings, their spouses, their children, or their friends. Even if Christianity helps us to love our families and our friends better than we would be able to apart from Christ, that kind of love is nevertheless common to all humankind.

So, John isn't talking about common love in this passage but about how God is the source of a particular love for a particular people. The Greek here is very specific. Lenski draws our attention to the fact that John is writing not about love in the abstract but specifically about *the* love (*he agape*): "The first fact is that 'this love is from God.' Note the [word *the*]. When our versions translate 'love is of God,' this is not exact.... Only '*the* love,' the one that John urges, the one of one Christian toward another, is from God."[1]

Recall that John did something similar in a previous passage when he wrote, "In this we have come to know *the* love, that he laid down his life for us, and we ought to lay down our lives for the brothers" (1 John 3:16). John was not talking about a generic kind of love but about *this* righteousness-love.[2] Here too, John is referring to a supernatural, sacrificial love of one Christian for another, a kind of love that flows only from the eternal life God gives to his children (1 John 3:14). This love is from God, and everyone who loves has been born of God and knows God.

Yes, God loves the whole world. Yes, God sends his rain to bless the just and the unjust alike (Matthew 5:43–48). Nevertheless, God bears a special love for his people, and he calls us to love one another in a manner that reflects his special love for his people. Paul makes a similar statement in Galatians 6:10: "So then, as we have opportunity, let us do good to everyone, and *especially to those who are of the household of faith.*" We are called to love and serve all people, but we are called to love and serve those who are of the household of faith in a special way. This doesn't lower the bar for the way in which we are called to love the world; instead, it raises the bar for the way in which we are to love our fellow brothers and sisters in Christ.

Second, John warns us that failing to love is incompatible with knowing God, because in fact "God is love" (1 John 4:8). In other words, God's identity is indistinguishable from his love. Love is not an optional, add-on feature to God, but rather, God is love.

Now, "love" can mean many things to many people, especially in our culture. Today, the world worships the idea that love can be whatever we make it to be. When we say that God is love, though, we are not allowed to project our own ideas of love onto God to define him. Instead, God is the one who defines love, because God is love. We cannot understand God from our own vague ideas about love; rather, we can only understand love by studying what God has revealed about himself in his word and in his Son Jesus Christ.

And very often, what God teaches us about himself will completely overturn our preconceptions about the nature of love. C. S. Lewis's surprising definition of "a loving God" is one of my favorites:

> You asked for a loving God: you have one. The great spirit you so lightly invoked, the "lord of terrible aspect," is present: not a senile benevolence that drowsily wishes you to be happy in your own way, not the cold philanthropy of a conscientious magistrate, nor the care of a host who feels responsible for the comfort of his guests, but the consuming fire Himself, the Love that made the worlds, persistent as the artist's love for his work and despotic as a man's love for a dog, provident and venerable as a father's love for a child, jealous, inexorable, exacting as love between the sexes.[3]

God's love lays a claim on our lives. Our own desires for God's love would mainly have him affirming us so that we could continue to do whatever we want to do because we want God's love to take away negative consequences for our actions. God's actual love toward us, however, refuses to leave us as loveless, selfish, cold creatures because he would be unloving to do so. Instead, God's love is exacting, jealous, and despotic in its demands, but only because God's love is infinitely gracious toward us.

The ultimate picture we have to illustrate the union of God's consuming jealousy with his perfect benevolence is the cross of Jesus. At the cross, God poured out on his own Son all his fury and wrath against our sin—that is, our offenses against God's love. God's wrath is not the opposite of God's love but the natural, righteous result of God's love against sin.

The doctrine of God's wrath is unpopular in our culture because we have a very low view of sin. We imagine the Bible is a rule book full of complicated, antiquated laws, and so we struggle to understand what we perceive to be God's disproportionate response when we stumble over a technicality here or there. If God flies off the handle for the smallest of offenses, we tell ourselves, then we are morally superior to God, with a better, more tolerant love. But remember what John wrote earlier: "If we say that we have not sinned, we make [God] a liar, and his word is not in us" (1 John 1:10).

We simply do not comprehend the horror of sin. Sin not only brings guilt, but it distorts our ability to see our own guilt, and so we do not fully recognize its ugliness. We fail to recognize the glorious beauty of God's perfect love, and we work hard to downplay the extent to which we have perpetrated evil against others, against ourselves, and even against God himself through our sin. Then, when God's righteous love opposes us in our sin, we shift into rejecting God's love outright.

What this also means is we do not understand God's love, and we do not understand God's wrath. Accordingly, John writes, "In this is the love, not that we have loved God, but that he has loved us and sent his Son to be the propitiation concerning our sins" (1 John 4:10). Again, John insists on this love that God demonstrated toward us at the cross of Jesus with the use of the emphatic word *the*: "In this is *the* love." John dismisses the value of what we call love so that he can reframe the discussion entirely.

Our love, John insists, is a poor imitation of the extraordinary love God has demonstrated toward us by sending his Son Jesus to the cross. We can talk all day about what good people we are, listing out all of our meager displays of "love," but John dismisses everything we have done (it is "not that we have loved God") by pointing to this third characteristic of God's love as the decisive proof that God is love: it is "that [God] has loved us and sent his Son to be the propitiation concerning our sins." The good news of the gospel is that God set aside his wrath against us by pouring it out on his own Son, making Jesus to be the atoning sacrifice for our sins.

And so, beloved, if God so loved us—as the source of love, as Love himself, and as the ultimate Lover who pursued us to the cross—then we also ought to love one another. God requires love from us not to burden us but because the entire nature of his relationship toward us is defined by his own great love.

ABIDING IN LOVE, ABIDING IN GOD

To summarize 1 John 4:7–12, then, John has laid out the obligation that we have as Jesus' disciples to love one another, on the basis of the love God has shown to us: "Beloved, if in this way God loved us, we also ought to love one another" (1 John 4:11). Based on the facts that God is the source of love, that God is Love himself, and that God demonstrated his great love toward us by sending Jesus to die on the cross for our sins, John insists we also ought to love, because "the one who does not love does not know God" (1 John 4:8).

Loving as God has loved us, however, is much easier said than done. How can we live up to such an overwhelming task? John explains:

> [13]In this we know that we abide in him and he in us, because he has given to us from his Spirit. [14]And we have seen and bear witness that the Father has sent the Son *to be* Savior of the world. [15]Whoever confesses that Jesus is the Son of God, in him God abides, and he in God. [16]And we have come to know and have believed the love that God has for us. God is love, and the one abiding in the love abides in God, and God abides in him. (1 John 4:13–16)

The only way to become someone who loves according to God's example is through an intimate, personal, living encounter with Love himself. Only by knowing Love close–up do we become lovers: "God is love, and the one abiding in the love abides in God, and God abides in him" (1 John 4:16).

Now, many people—Christians and non-Christians alike—rightly believe that love is important; however, the more important question is not whether someone believes in love but rather how someone suggests we accomplish that goal of loving one another as God has loved us. At first glance, love seems so straightforward that we are tempted to skip right over John's message that we cannot love unless we "abide in God." But apart from God, we have no access to God's love.

John is again teaching us that we must abide in God. We talked previously about John's use of the word *abide* in chapter 5, looking at 1 John 2:28: "And now, little children, abide in him." Now, in 1 John 4:13–16, John spirals in closer to what it means to "abide in God."

Here, John tells us that abiding in God is primarily a theological issue. John writes, "Whoever confesses that Jesus is the Son of God, in him God abides, and he in God" (1 John 4:15). John has already railed against those who deny that Jesus is the Son of God (1 John 2:22–23), as well as against those who deny that the Son became human (1 John 4:2–3), and here he reiterates what he has already said: those who abide in Christ (the true disciples of Jesus) freely confess that the human Jesus is the Son of God.

But this isn't a dry, academic lecture on theology. In this phrase, John is exposing the vital connection between right doctrine and right living—that is, between good theology and loving one another as God has loved us. God abides only in those who rightly confess Jesus as the Son of God who was sent to be the Savior of humankind, and only those who confess this about Jesus abide in God. Therefore, our ability to love—which requires our abiding in God, and God's abiding in us—depends on sound theology. Look at the repeated phrases in verses 15 and 16:

> [15]Whoever confesses that Jesus is the Son of God, *in him God abides, and he in God.* [16]And we have come to know and have believed the love that God has for us.

God is love, and *the one abiding in the love abides in God, and God abides in him.*

Christian discipleship does not force us to choose between good theology and love. John is telling us here that love is impossible apart from good theology, and that good theology necessarily leads to love.

Careful reading of this passage, though, raises one more question: If our ability to love depends on sound theology, then where does our theology come from? John actually has answered this question already in verse 13, where he unfolds the main theme of this passage: "In this we know that we abide in him and he in us, because he has given to us from his Spirit." Our ability to confess Christ—as well as our ability to love—requires the transforming power of the Holy Spirit.

On this, Colin Kruse writes:

> Within this letter the role of the Spirit is always related to the truth about Jesus Christ. If we take note of the role of the Spirit in the rest of the letter, we have to conclude that it is neither the very presence of the Spirit nor the activity of the Spirit producing love for fellow believers that the author has in mind here, but rather the Spirit as witness to the truth about Jesus proclaimed by the eyewitnesses (cf. 2:18–27; 3:24b–4:6; 5:6–8).... What the author is implying in 4:13, then, is that because the Spirit teaches believers about the love of God expressed in the sending of the Son to be the Saviour of the world (4:14), and because they believe that teaching, they may be assured that they dwell in God and God in them.[4]

We do not believe because we are smarter, more spiritually sensitive, or clearer thinkers than other people; we believe because the Spirit personally takes us to be his pupils and because he gently, graciously, and clearly teaches us about the love the Father has for us in Christ Jesus. And when we see the love of God—genuinely see it, love it, and believe in it, with humility, repentance, and joy—our lives are transformed through the gospel.

Though it seems so simple for someone to believe in Christ Jesus for salvation, such an act actually requires a miracle of God in our hearts. But the gospel is that the same God who created the entire cosmos now creates life, faith, and love in our cold, unbelieving, unloving hearts.

The Apostle Paul, in a letter to the church in Corinth, writes this about his fellow Israelites who were continuing to reject Christ:

> [3:14]But their minds were hardened. For to this day, when they read the old covenant, the same veil remains unlifted, because only through Christ is it taken away. [15]Yes, to this day whenever Moses is read a veil lies over their hearts. [16]But when one turns to the Lord, the veil is removed. [17]*Now the Lord is the Spirit, and where the Spirit of the Lord is, there is freedom.* [18]And we all, with unveiled face, beholding the glory of the Lord, are being transformed into the same image from one degree of glory to another. *For this comes from the Lord who is the Spirit....* [4:6]For God, who said, "Let light shine out of darkness," has shone in our hearts to give the light of the knowledge of the glory of God in the face of Jesus Christ. (2 Corinthians 3:14–18, 4:6)

The Holy Spirit is the Lord who gives freedom to those who are in bondage to sin, with a veil covering their hearts from seeing the glory of the Lord. The Spirit is the one who pierces the veil to enter our hearts directly, shining the light of the knowledge of the glory of God in the face of Jesus Christ. Then, as the Spirit teaches us about the beauty and glory of the crucified and resurrected God-man Jesus Christ, we turn to the Lord, and the veil is removed, so we are transformed into Christ's image from one degree of glory to another as we continue to abide in him.

PERFECT LOVE DRIVES OUT FEAR

At this point, John ties together our growth in love with the hope of the gospel:

> [17]In this the love has been perfected with us, so that we may have confidence in the day of judgment, for just as he is, so also we are in this world. [18]Fear is not in love, but perfect love drives out fear, for fear involves punishment, but the one who fears has not been perfected in love. [19]We love because he has first loved us. [20]If someone says, "I love God," but he hates his brother, he is a liar: for the one who does not love his brother whom he has seen cannot love God, whom he has not seen. [21]And this command we have from him, that the one who loves God should also love his brother. (1 John 4:17–21)

As he had done in chapter 2, verse 28 ("And now, little children, abide in him, so that when he is manifested we may have complete confidence and not shrink in shame from him at his coming"), John points to the day of Christ's return as a day of judgment to be feared by those who do not abide in him. As he had also done in that verse, John here stresses the confidence believers should have for the day of judgment. But what is the basis of our confidence? Or specifically, how do we know whether we are among those who have confidence in Christ? When John writes that "perfect love drives out fear" and that "the one who fears has not been perfected in love," he is explaining that love is evidence of God's work in our lives: "In this the love has been perfected with us, so that we may have confidence in the day of judgment, for just as he is, so also we are in this world" (1 John 4:17). If God has begun the process of perfecting his love in us (even though we will still fall short of God's own perfect standard of love), we may have absolute confidence for the day of judgment, because as Christ is, so also are we in the world. In other words, just as Jesus cannot be condemned now that he has risen from the dead in victory over sin, we who abide in him by faith cannot be condemned either.

This love, then, is the link between verses 17 and 18 and 19 to 21. Love is the evidence of God's saving work in our lives (and therefore the evidence of our eternal confidence), and so love is the expectation and goal for Christian conduct. At first it seems as though John is abruptly changing the subject in verse 19, but he is simply extending his logic. If love is our confidence for the day of judgment, then Christians ought to take love seriously in our daily lives. Those who say they love God but yet hate their fellow believers are liars, and because they do not love, they have no reason for confidence on the last day.

John is challenging us to honestly evaluate the evidence of our salvation. Is the fruit of love present in our interactions toward those others for whom Jesus Christ has died? If not, then shouldn't that suggest to us that we do not know God (1 John 4:8)? If we cannot love someone who bears God's image, then how can we imagine we love the origin of that image?

And so beloved, let us love one another, for the love is from God, and everyone who loves has been born of God and knows God.

QUESTIONS FOR REFLECTION

1. If you were going to describe God's love to someone else, what would you say? How would your description align with what John describes in this passage? How would your description align with the example of Jesus dying on the cross?
2. How does a full understanding of the nature of sin change the way we view God's love in comparison to our own love?
3. What role does the Holy Spirit play in your salvation? How aware are you of his presence?

9
Faith

1 John 5:1–12

We closed the previous chapter with words from 1 John 4:7: "Beloved, let us love one another, for the love is from God, and everyone who loves has been born of God and knows God." This kind of supernatural love, John explains, is something that comes only from God. So, those who act out this kind of love show evidence that they have been born of God and that they know God. The opposite statement is also true: whoever does not love has not been born of God and does not know God.

Love comes only from God. There is no way to produce love in your own life apart from the omnipotent power of the Holy Spirit's ministry, as he shines light on the gospel of Jesus, illuminating Christ's beauty so that you cannot help but to look upon Jesus, believe in him, and be saved. From there, the gracious, life-giving Spirit only continues his work to produce love in your life, causing the roots of the gospel to grow deeper and deeper into your heart.

But what about faith? Where does it come from? Based on what the Apostle John has just written, we can agree that love comes from God, but where does our faith come from? Is faith the piece that we bring to the table, our own small contribution that gives God formal permission to begin applying his work of salvation in our lives? Or, does faith also come from God, in the same way that love comes from God?

Now, the Scriptures are very clear that salvation comes only by faith and not by anything good we ourselves do. The Apostle Paul is especially insistent on this point:

> Yet we know that a person is not justified by works of the law but through faith in Jesus Christ, so we also have believed in Christ Jesus, in order to be justified by faith in Christ and not by works of the law, because by works of the law no one will be justified. (Galatians 2:16)

> For by grace you have been saved through faith. And this is not your own doing; it is the gift of God, not a result of works, so that no one may boast. (Ephesians 2:8–9)

But what isn't so clear from these passages is the question of where our faith comes from. Look again at Ephesians 2:8–9, and notice the second sentence: "And this is not your own doing; it is the gift of God." What exactly is Paul referring to when he says, "this is not your own doing; it is the gift of God"? If he is only talking about the phrase "For by grace you have been saved," then his writing is redundant, since salvation "by grace" is by definition a gift of God, and not our own doing.

In the context, then, the best explanation is that Paul is referring to salvation as well as to the phrase "through faith." Paul is teaching here that the whole work of salvation—including our faith, as well as our love—comes as a gift of God and is not something that we produce independently from God. Through some mystery, God graciously gives even our faith to us as a loving gift.

Now, let's return to our study in 1 John. The apostle picks up the same themes in 1 John 5:1–12 as he continues to spiral toward the climax of his letter. In the first five verses of this passage, John offers the clearest, most concise summary of his theology in all of 1 John:

> [1]Everyone who believes that Jesus is the Christ has been born of God, and everyone who loves the Father loves *whoever* has been born of him. [2]In this we know that we love the children of God, whenever we love God and obey his commandments. [3]For this is the love of God, that we keep his commandments, and his commandments are not burdensome. [4]For everyone who has been born of God overcomes the world, and this is the victory that overcame the world: our faith. [5]But who is the one who overcomes the world if not the one who believes that Jesus is the Son of God? (1 John 5:1–5)

John has already written about believing in Jesus as the Christ and the Son of God, loving the brethren, and keeping the commandments, but he does something different from the rest of his letter here: (1) he shows how these virtues all stem from our being born of God; and (2) he describes these virtues as a great victory over the world.

THE NEW BIRTH

John attributes both faith and love to the miraculous power of the new birth, what theologians sometimes call "regeneration." Note the tenses at work in verse 1: "Everyone who believes [present] that Jesus is the Christ has been born [present perfect] of God." If someone believes now, it is because that person has (already) been born of God. Faith comes as a result of new birth. As John Stott explains in his commentary, "believing is the consequence, not the cause, of the new birth."[1]

John Murray explains this concept more fully:

> Regeneration is the beginning of all saving grace in us, and all saving grace in exercise on our part proceeds from the fountain of regeneration. We are not born again by faith or repentance or conversion; we repent and believe because we have been regenerated....

The embrace of Christ in faith is the first evidence of regeneration and only thus may we know that we have been regenerated.[2]

Regeneration (the new birth) is the fountainhead of our salvation. As Murray notes, we repent and believe because God has begun a new work in us through regeneration. Faith, then, is the first sign that God has given us new birth.

This was also how John wrote about love in the previous passage in 1 John 4:7: "everyone who loves has been born of God." Just as it is impossible to love apart from being born of God, so it is impossible to believe that Jesus is the Christ apart from being born of God. To paraphrase John Stott, love (like faith) is the consequence and not the cause of the new birth.

Recall that John had previously written about being born of God in a passage about our hope in Christ:

> 2:29If you know that he is righteous, you know also that everyone practicing righteousness *has been born of him.* 3:1See what kind of love the Father has given to us, *that we might be called children of God,* and we are!... 2Beloved, *now we are children of God,* but it has not yet been manifested what we will be. We know know that when he appears, we will be like him, for we will see him as he is. 3And everyone hoping in him purifies himself, just as he is pure.... 9*Everyone having been born of God does not practice sin,* for his seed abides in him, and he is not able to practice sin, *for he has been born of God.* 10In this is manifest who are *the children of God* and who are the children of the devil: everyone not practicing righteousness *is not of God* ["of God" is short for "born of God"], nor the one not loving his brother. (1 John 2:29–3:10)

The new birth, as John explains it, causes a radical departure from our old lives. Where we formerly lived in sin and hatred, we now practice righteousness and love our fellow believers. Of course, we don't do these things perfectly all the time, but God's "seed abides in" us in such a way that keeps drawing us back to God, repenting from our sins and believing the gospel, learning to love others more and more.

John also talks in this passage about keeping God's commandments, but it's clear he is thinking primarily of the commandment to love: "For this is the love of God, that we keep his commandments" (1 John 5:3). Do you remember all the way back to 1 John 2:7–11? There, John explained that the old commandment they had heard from the beginning had become a new commandment in Jesus—and that the old commandment Jesus made new was the commandment to love: "The one who loves his brother abides in the light and in him is not a stumbling block" (1 John 2:10).

So, when John tells us that "his commandments are not burdensome" (1 John 5:3), we understand what he means: our new birth supplies us all the power of the Holy Spirit to obey God's commandments. Of course, obeying God will be challenging, but because we have been born of God and are no longer the children of the devil (1 John 3:10), keeping God's commandments is no longer something that is completely against our nature.

THE VICTORY OF BEING BORN OF GOD

As John continues to describe this radical life transformation, he calls the new birth "the victory that overcame the world" in 1 John 5:4. The word for "victory" (and also for "overcome") is *nike*, a word that the Greeks used as the name of the winged goddess of victory, Nike. (The shoe company is named after this Greek goddess, and the company's swoosh logo is meant to represent the goddess Nike's wings.) John uses the word four times in 1 John 5:4–5: "For everyone who has been born of God overcomes [*nika*] the world, and this is the victory [*nike*] that overcame [*nikesasa*] the world: our faith. But who is the one who overcomes [*nikon*] the world if not the one who believes that Jesus is the Son of God?" Our victory is the greatest of all victories. Alexander the Great probably got the farthest in conquering the world through his great military victories across Europe, Africa, and Asia, but even he died before he could overcome the whole world. Yet John writes here that even the humblest, smallest, weakest child who believes upon Jesus has overcome the entire world.

How? By faith. Specifically, by faith that Jesus is the Christ (1 John 5:1) and that Jesus is the eternal Son of God (1 John 5:5). John had previously insisted that Jesus is the Christ and the Son of God in 1 John 2:22–24:

> ²²Who is the liar except the one who denies that Jesus is the Christ? This one is the antichrist, the one who denies the Father and the Son. ²³Everyone who denies the Son does not have the Father either; the one who confesses the Son has the Father also. ²⁴As for you, let what you heard from the beginning abide in you. If what you heard from the beginning abides in you, you will also abide in the Son and in the Father.

Anyone who grasps the significance of these statements does so only because God has graciously given them new birth, and a new life—a new life defined by the person of Jesus Christ, the Son of God.

No one, apart from the work of the Holy Spirit to grant us the new birth, could possibly embrace these thoughts because they are so foolish to human wisdom. Jesus of Nazareth is the Christ and the Son of God? Jesus, born out of wedlock to a poor, teenage girl? Jesus, condemned for blasphemy and cursed by God as he died on a tree? This Jesus is the Son of God and the Anointed Christ of God?

Only the new birth can overcome the skepticism of this world in order to believe in Jesus wholeheartedly—just as only the new birth can grant us love for one another and create obedient hearts. Everyone who believes, who loves, and who obeys—that is, everyone who has victory over the world—has undoubtedly been born of God.

THERE ARE THREE THAT TESTIFY

Even though Christians experience a victorious new birth, being born of God himself, in order to believe, love, and obey, we still continue to wrestle throughout our lives with the question of why we believe, love, and obey. Does our faith rest on some kind of psychological deception, whether from an over–emotionalized experience, a desperately guilty conscience, or some kind of longing for an absent father figure? Deep down, are we loving other Christians simply to gain power, influence, and maybe even money from those we pretend to love? Does our obedience spring from nothing more than a desire to lift ourselves up and put others down on the basis of self–righteous legalism? And if not, what makes our own faith, love, and obedience legitimate?

John addresses our questions concerning the reality of Jesus by pointing us to the testimony of the "three that testify," water, blood, and the Spirit. He writes:

> [6]This is the one who came by water and blood: Jesus Christ—not in the water only but in the water and in the blood. And the Spirit is the one who gives testimony, for the Spirit is the Truth. [7]For there are three who give testimony, [8]the Spirit and the water and the blood, and these three agree [lit., "the three are unto the one"]. (1 John 5:6–8)

The reason our new birth is a victory and not a mind–washing defeat is that the new birth frees us from our sin–imposed blindness to see and love the truth about Jesus, especially as we consider the testimony of the witnesses he calls forward.

Now, John is not entirely clear about the precise meaning of his witnesses. In fact, verse 6 is one of the more controversial verses in the Bible because John does not explicitly spell out what the water and the blood signify, even if "the Spirit" clearly refers to the Holy Spirit. Adding further confusion, the King James Version of the Bible unfortunately follows a bad textual source, so that verses 7–8 say this:

> [7]For there are three that bear record in heaven, the Father, the Word, and the Holy Ghost: and these three are one. [8]And there are three that bear witness in earth, the Spirit, and the water, and the blood: and these three agree in one. (1 John 5:7–8 KJV)

Despite the fact that verse 7 in the KJV expounds good trinitarian theology, it isn't what John wrote. The addition of "the Father, the Word, and the Holy Ghost" doesn't "appear in a single Greek manuscript of the New Testament prior to about 1520," over fourteen hundred years after John wrote his letter.[3]

So, what is John's purpose in citing the water, the blood, and the Spirit? If we look closely at what John writes, we can find clues. It seems that water (whatever water might mean) was not the disputed witness, for Jesus Christ came "not in the water only but in the water and the blood." From this, it sounds as though the people against whom John is writing wanted to focus exclusively on the water, ignoring the witness of the blood. John insists, though, that Jesus did not come *only* in the water but in the water *and* the blood.

John's contested witness, then, is "the blood." John had written about the blood of Jesus before, telling us that it is Jesus' blood that cleanses us from all sin (1 John 1:7). Additionally, when John speaks of Jesus as the propitiation for our sins (1 John 2:2, 4:10), he is making reference to the blood sacrifice of Jesus that is effective for the forgiveness of our sins. The blood of Jesus represents our Lord's suffering, crucifixion, and death, and John is insisting on its testimony for his case.

The best explanation of what the water and the blood mean here, then, is that many false teachers (the antichrists; 1 John 2:18–27) had been preaching that the divine Christ descended upon the human Jesus at the baptism and then departed from Jesus before the cross. The problem in John's day was not so much that people were challenging the divinity of Jesus (although some challenged Jesus' relationship as the Son to the Father) but that they were challenging his full humanity. How could God actually become a human? If *this* Jesus actually shed fully human blood for us, then the antichrists lose their case.

The Gospels, however, point with a unified voice to the full humanity and the full deity of Jesus. He was not a god who only seemed human, and he was not a human who lied about being God. Instead, we read that the Father bore witness concerning the Son at Jesus' baptism (the water): "This is my beloved Son, with whom I am well pleased" (Matthew 3:17; see also Mark 1:11, Luke 3:22, John 1:32–34). The accounts of the four Gospels have slight variations, as each writer brings out a different aspect of Jesus' baptism, but they all agree in testifying that Jesus is the Son of God, in whom the Father is well pleased.

The accounts of the crucifixion (the blood) have a bit more variation; however, all of them also testify that this Jesus dying on the cross was still the Son of God—the Divine Christ had not somehow left the man Jesus, as the antichrists suggested. In the accounts of Matthew 27:54 and Mark 15:39, the Roman centurion and those with him seeing Jesus die were compelled to declare, "Truly this man was the Son of God!" In Luke 23:40–42, one of the criminals crucified next to Jesus recognizes that Jesus has done nothing wrong and asks Jesus to remember him when Jesus comes into his kingdom. Then, Luke also records that the centurion declares, "Certainly this man was innocent!" (Luke 23:47). Keep in mind that the charges against Jesus were for blasphemy by claiming to be the Son of God (Luke 22:70–71). For the thief on the cross and the centurion to claim that Jesus was innocent is a roundabout way of affirming, along with the accounts recorded in Matthew and in Mark, that Jesus is the Son of God.

The account in the Gospel of John (written by the same Apostle John who wrote the letter we are studying) is the most interesting of the four. John writes:

> [31]Since it was the day of Preparation, and so that the bodies would not remain on the cross on the Sabbath (for that Sabbath was a high day), the Jews asked Pilate that their legs might be broken and that they might be taken away. [32]So the soldiers came and broke the legs of the first, and of the other who had been crucified with him. [33]But when they came to Jesus and saw that he was already dead, they did not break his legs. [34]But one of the soldiers pierced his side with a spear, *and at once there came out blood and water.* [35]*He who saw it has borne witness—his testimony is true,* and he knows that he is telling the truth—that you also may believe. (John 19:31–35)

Some people think the Apostle John is referring in 1 John 5:6–7 to the blood and water that came from the side of Jesus, since the language is so similar; however, if this were the case, it is difficult to see how anyone could believe that Jesus came by the water but not the blood: "This is the one who came by water and blood: Jesus Christ—*not in the water only* but in the water and in the blood" (1 John 5:6).

The better explanation, then, is that John recorded the physical outpouring of water and blood from the side of Jesus in his Gospel as a true, vivid illustration to confirm that Jesus had indeed come both by water at his baptism and by blood at his crucifixion. Notice that immediately after John mentions the flow of blood and water in John 19:35, he insists that he has given eyewitness testimony that is true (and he knows that he is telling the truth!) so that you, the reader, may also believe. This isn't a free-association game in John's mind but an insight that came from the inspiration of the Holy Spirit to shed light on the meaning of what John physically saw as an eyewitness at the cross. The Son of God had come by the water and the blood, and any spirit that does not confess Jesus

Christ having-come-in-flesh is not from God but is the spirit of the antichrist (1 John 4:2–3).

WHOEVER HAS THE SON HAS LIFE

But one witness remains: the Spirit. In fact, John has more to say about the Spirit than he does about the water and the blood combined. So, what is the Spirit's testimony? How does he enhance the testimony of the water and the blood? He writes:

> [7]For there are three who give testimony, [8]the Spirit and the water and the blood, and these three agree. [9]If we receive the testimony of men, the testimony of God is greater. For this is the testimony of God that he has given testimony concerning his Son. [10]The one who believes in the Son of God has the testimony in himself; the one who does not believe in God has made him a liar, for he has not believed in the testimony which God has given concerning his Son. [11]And this is the testimony, that God has given eternal life to us, and this life is in his Son. [12]The one who has the Son has the life; the one who does not have the Son of God does not have life. (1 John 5:7–12)

First, John reminds us that we dare not oppose the testimony of the Spirit, because the Spirit who testifies is himself God: "If we receive the testimony of men, the testimony of God is greater. For this is the testimony of God that he has given testimony concerning his Son.... [T]he one who does not believe in God has made him a liar, for he has not believed in the testimony which God has given concerning his Son" (1 John 5:9, 10).

The Holy Spirit is the third person of the Trinity, sharing the same divine nature with the Father and the Son but at the same time a distinct person from the Father and the Son. The Father, Son, and Holy Spirit are three persons but one God— not three gods and not a single person who manifests himself in different ways at different times (here as the Father, there as the Son, and now as the Holy Spirit), but three persons who exist in relationship together as one God. This doctrine of the Trinity is beyond our ability to understand fully, but yet the Scriptures reveal again and again that there is only one God and that this God reveals himself as three distinct persons.

Second, John does not say here that the Holy Spirit testifies by working through rational, point-by-point reasoning to persuade our minds logically. In other words, the Spirit does not come to us saying, "Here are the five reasons you ought to believe that the man Jesus is the Son of God." Now, this doesn't mean that Christianity is an illogical religion. God invented reason, and God does reason with us logically through his word. Paul's letter to the Romans, for example, is a masterpiece of Christian logic.

But John is saying here that the Spirit offers something other than a purely logical testimony by appealing to us through our minds. In fact, the testimony of the Spirit is more direct than that: "The one who believes in the Son of God *has the testimony in himself*" (1 John 5:10). We receive the Spirit's testimony internally, not as something that comes to us from an outside source. So, the testimony we receive from the Spirit does not consist of raw facts nor of an aesthetically beautiful faith system nor of emotionally pleasing feelings. We do not receive the testimony, evaluate it, and then decide whether we like it.

Instead, John explains to us that the Spirit's testimony is life itself: "And this is the testimony, that God has given eternal life to us, and this life is in his Son" (1 John 5:11). God's testimony, John explains, works like this: We, like Lazarus, lie dead in the tomb. We have been swallowed up by the grave because of our sins, without any hope of recovery. The Holy Spirit, like Jesus in front of his friend's tomb, proclaims, "Lazarus, come out!" By this extraordinary, life-giving testimony of the Holy Spirit, we are born of God in a moment to new, eternal life—as well as to new faith, new love, and new obedience. Now that we are alive, we cannot help but to believe that Jesus is the Son of God and to love fellow believers—all because the Holy Spirit has testified us back to life.

This eternal life, however, is not independent or stand-alone. We cannot take eternal life as an acquired possession and then go back to our old ways of living apart from God. Instead, eternal life is wrapped up in Jesus Christ: "and this life is in his Son. The one who has the Son has the life; the one who does not have the Son of God does not have life" (1 John 5:11b–12). In fact, *this* Jesus—the Son of God who came in the flesh—is himself the eternal life given to us by the testimony of the Spirit.

If you have Jesus, you have life—in fact, you also have, along with Christ, the testimony of the Spirit, the new birth, the faith, the love, and the obedience. The Spirit bears witness to Jesus, and the Spirit's life-giving testimony is Jesus—not merely a message about Jesus or an argument for Jesus, but *Jesus himself* in all his glory.

Our new faith is not an intellectual decision we come to independently, through our own reasoning; it is the natural result of our new birth when the Holy Spirit gives us Jesus. Our new love is not something we begin to try really hard to do, attempting to imitate what Jesus demonstrated perfectly when he died on the cross; instead, Jesus made the old commandment to love one another radically new by giving us life itself through the gospel. The obedience commanded by God's law becomes simple in Jesus—we learn to obey as the Spirit gives us more and more of Jesus.

But if you do not have the Son of God, you have nothing. On behalf of Christ, by the mercy of the Father, according to the life-giving testimony of the Spirit, I plead with you: Be reconciled to God through Jesus Christ. Do not harden your dead heart any longer against the life that is in Jesus Christ. Embrace him by faith.

The one who has the Son has the life; the one who does not have the Son of God does not have life.

QUESTIONS FOR REFLECTION

1. What surprises you most about what John teaches us regarding the new birth?
2. How should it affect our evangelism if the chief witness the Holy Spirit uses to convince people to believe in Jesus is life and not logical arguments?
3. If you are honest, do you place more value on the benefits we gain from Jesus (forgiveness of sins, social standing, better friendships/marriages/parenting/ jobs, etc.) or on the fullness of life we experience through knowing Jesus?

10
Prayer

1 John 5:13–17

J ohn's first letter—the letter we are studying in this book—does not stand alone. John wrote another book called the Gospel of John, and the two need to be read together. The Gospel of John and the First Letter of John are unified in their message and theology, but John writes each with a different purpose in mind. Taken together, John's Gospel and his first letter complement and reinforce each other.

If you remember from all the way back in the introduction to this book, we looked at how John's primary goal in his Gospel is to evangelize—that is, to tell the good news of Jesus to people who do not yet believe. He does not reveal this purpose until near the very end of his Gospel, where he writes the following:

> [30]Now Jesus did many other signs in the presence of the disciples, which are not written in this book; [31]but these are written *so that you may believe that Jesus is the Christ, the Son of God, and that by believing you may have life in his name.*(John 20:30–31)

So, John tells us that his purpose for writing this Gospel was to introduce us to Jesus as the Christ and the Son of God so that by believing in Jesus, we may have life in his name. For this reason, the Gospel of John narrates the story of Jesus, telling us about his disciples, his teachings, his miracles, his enemies, his crucifixion, his death, and his resurrection— everything we need to know and believe to be saved.

John wrote this letter, however, for a different purpose. Instead of writing a letter to evangelize those who do not yet believe, he wrote it to perfect and strengthen the faith of those who already believe in Jesus. As in his Gospel, the Apostle John does not reveal his purpose for writing until the end of 1 John. Here, John uses strikingly similar terms to what he wrote in his purpose statement from the Gospel of John:

> These things I wrote to you so that you may know that you have eternal life, to those of you who believe in the name of the Son of God. (1 John 5:13)

John's Gospel was written "so that you may believe that Jesus is the Christ, the Son of God," but John's letter was written "to those of you who believe in the name of the Son of God." The goal of John's Gospel was "that by believing you may have life in his name," but John's letter was written "that you may know that you have eternal life."

In other words, the Apostle John wrote 1 John as a primer for disciples. His goal in this letter is to help people know and love Jesus better who already believe that he is the Christ, the Son of God, so the entire letter is filled with warnings against falling away and instructions on how Christians ought to behave on the basis of the love of God we have already come to know.

This doesn't mean 1 John has no value for non-Christians. I have personally seen someone come to know Jesus through studying 1 John. Because of the way 1 John gives such a clear picture of what lifelong, faithful discipleship after Jesus should look like, people who do not yet believe in Jesus can learn a lot about Christianity from studying this letter. Likewise, the Gospel of John has extraordinary relevance for disciples of

Jesus, so it's important we don't make the mistake of pushing this generalization too far.

What this means, though, is that all the subjects John tackles in 1 John—his explanation of the gospel, his instructions about love, his insistence on truth, and even his encouragements about perseverance, persecution, and discernment—have been written to teach those of us who believe in the name of the Son of God that we indeed have eternal life. John has a practical purpose in mind for gaining this knowledge, but for now, let's take a closer look at what John is telling us in verse 13.

CONFIDENCE IN ETERNAL LIFE

Eternal life is a serious matter to John. He does not promise it to everyone claiming any kind of affiliation with Christianity at all but only to believers in the name of the Son of God. John has no tolerance for a vague, Christian-ish faith. In the previous verse, John had just written, "The one who has the Son has the life; the one who does not have the Son of God does not have life" (1 John 5:12), and he means it. Only in the Son do we find life, and only in his name do we find salvation.

When the biblical writers talk about the "name" of God, they are referring to his reputation, his character, and his deeds. Most of all, they are talking about the way in which God demonstrated his free grace, love, and mercy toward us. God so loved the world, the Scriptures tell us, that he fulfilled his ancient promise to save his people by nothing short of sending his own Son into the world to die for our sins and to rise from the dead in victory over sin, death, and the devil. Jesus has now received all authority in heaven and on earth, and he reigns at the right hand of his Father in heaven. John's phrase "the name of the Son of God" here is a reference to this full gospel message.

This is one of the reasons I love 1 John so much: the apostle holds the gospel of Jesus high throughout his entire letter. Everything he writes points us to Jesus, the eternal Son of the Father who became man, whose blood was shed to cleanse us from our sins. The Son of God actually became the sacrificial appeasement to his Father for us so that we would escape condemnation! The Son of God himself drank his Father's foaming cup of wrath, and in doing so he gave up his own life so that we could live.

The one who has the Son has life.

This doctrine is not something reserved for uptight, dry theologians to write boring books about it. Rather, this is the message that embodies all of our hope and confidence in this life and the next.

And so, John is writing so that those of us who believe in the name of the Son of God (i.e., we who believe the gospel) may know that we have eternal life. John wants us to have a deep, confident, joyful knowledge that the eternal life Jesus offers is ours through faith, despite the fact that all through this letter, he has written several statements that very possibly might cause us to doubt our salvation: "The one practicing sin is from the devil, for from the beginning the devil has been sinning" (1 John 3:8); "But whoever has the livelihood of the world and sees his brother having need and closes his heart from him, how does the love of God abide in him?" (1 John 3:17); "If someone says, 'I love God,' but he hates his brother, he is a liar: for the one who does not love his brother whom he has seen cannot love God, whom he has not seen" (1 John 4:20). Who could measure up to such high standards?

But in 1 John 5:13, the apostle is explaining that he has not written those warnings to cause believers to doubt. Instead, he writes these things so that we who believe in the name of the Son of God may know we have eternal life. He wants to give us assurance of our salvation and our eternal life! In the face of the antichrists who preach a different, false gospel, John wants us to know with certainty that we may find restful, confident assurance by putting our faith in Jesus as the Christ, the Son of God.

So, we need to hear John's message of gospel comfort in

this passage. If you are someone who struggles with assurance so that you cannot seem to get the doubting feelings of your heart to line up with the gospel's promise that Jesus loves you, then these verses are for you: "The one who has the Son has the life; the one who does not have the Son of God does not have life. These things I wrote to you so that you may know that you have eternal life, to those of you who believe in the name of the Son of God" (1 John 5:12–13). Meditate upon these verses and claim them through faith. Believe the promise that if you have the Son of God, you do have life—even eternal life! Satan wants you to wander around endlessly in your doubts, because through doubt he can take your eyes off of Jesus and destroy you in your despair.

The truth of the gospel is this: you have never been—and you will never be—worthy of the salvation Jesus offers, and yet Jesus has made you worthy through his own worthiness. Stop trying to find something of your own that you can offer to God in the hopes that he will accept you. If you have Jesus, then you have eternal life, because whoever has the Son has life.

CONFIDENCE LEADS TO PRAYER

After assuring his readers that he has written his letter to confirm that they have eternal life if they believe in the name of the Son of God, John begins to unfold what this confidence looks like, practically speaking:

> ¹⁴And this is the confidence that we have toward him, that if we ask something according to his will, he hears us. ¹⁵And if we have come to know that he hears us *in* whatever we ask, *then* we have come to know that we have the requests that we have asked from him. (1 John 5:14–15)

John wants us to see prayer as the practical result of our confidence. A confident Christian is not arrogant or dismissive of people who do not yet believe in Jesus. A confident Christian is a praying Christian. If we genuinely believe we have life in the Son of God, then we will claim, utilize, and depend upon that life in Christ through our communion with him in prayer.

We often struggle to understand this principle because we share a common misconception about prayer. Too often, we think about prayer almost exclusively in terms of asking for a list of things—finding a new job, being healed from a sickness, discerning God's will for our lives, and so on. It is not wrong to ask for any of those things, but the confident prayer that John writes about here is so much more than that.

Prayer is not a spiritual shopping list. Prayer is direct access into the throne room of God Almighty in the highest heavens. Our prayers bring us into true worship. Through prayer, we request and receive forgiveness, according to the shed blood and righteousness of Jesus Christ. In prayer, we plead for God's kingdom to come to earth, as in heaven. Prayer brings us into close communion with God so that we can pray in boldness, joy, and purpose, knowing that God has made us alive to such a privileged life of prayer. We are no longer slaves who merely do God's bidding but friends who may petition God to intervene in this world—and by doing so, we could alter the course of history.

John does not give us a blank check to ask for anything that our selfish hearts might desire. Our confidence is a great privilege that we should never abuse. Instead, John promises us that "if we ask something according to his will, he hears us" (verse 14). The confidence we have before God gives us the right to pray according to God's will, and not according to our own will.

So, how do we go about determining God's will in our prayers? We shouldn't go to the opposite extreme of fearful paralysis as we wait to discern God's will perfectly before coming to him in prayer, because prayer is the place where God teaches us his will. John Stott helpfully explains:

Prayer is not a convenient device for imposing our will upon God, or bending His will to ours, but the prescribed way of subordinating our will to His. It is by prayer that we seek God's will, embrace it and align ourselves with it. Every true prayer is a variation on the theme "Thy will be done."[1]

Part of our confidence is that God will not abandon us to our sinful, selfish cravings but that he will actually transform our hearts while we pray, teaching us more and more to love the life that is in the Son of God. Just as my wife and I have to train our young children not to eat rocks on the playground but to enjoy a balanced diet of good foods instead, so also God is training us to desire and to pray for things that are truly good.

And as God teaches us to pray according to his will, we learn to pray with confidence that God will unwaveringly grant us what we ask according to his will. God loves to give good gifts to his children, and God gives us prayer not only so we can ask for and receive God's good gifts but also so he can teach us what to ask for in the first place.

PRAYING FOR THE PRODIGAL BROTHER

In 1 John 5:13–15, John has so far explained that the confidence we have about our eternal life ought to translate into prayer. Now, in verses 16–17, John gives us a specific application for this prayer:

> [16]If someone sees his brother sinning a sin not *leading* to death, he shall ask, and he shall give him life, to those *whose* sinning *does* not *lead* toward death. *There* is a sin *leading* toward death; I do not say that he should pray concerning this. [17]All unrighteousness is sin, and *there* is a sin not *leading* toward death. (1 John 5:16–17)

Here, John applies the general principle of prayer to a specific prayer for reclaiming a wandering, prodigal brother. John always uses "brother" to refer to a believer in his letter, and so the situation John has in mind here describes one believer observing a fellow believer who is falling into sin. The believer who observes his brother's sin should neither resort to gossip nor ignore what is happening. Instead, he or she should pray for the wandering believer with the confidence and assurance that God will restore life, faith, and obedience to this prodigal.

Praying for someone who begins heading down a path toward sin is a fairly natural response for believers. It is frustrating and painful to see a fellow believer starting to choose sin over Jesus. Suddenly, we realize how incapable we are of altering the course of someone who is pursuing hard after sin. Only God's Holy Spirit can change hearts, so we have no choice but to pray once a fellow believer's sin is exposed.

This is where the context of this passage is important: John is writing about confident prayer. We are not praying to a god that we otherwise do not know, hoping against hope that someone, somewhere will hear us and answer our prayers. Again, this doesn't mean God will do everything we ask him to in the exact way we ask him to do it. Rather, it means we are praying to the God who loves us and who has granted us eternal life, even though granting us eternal life meant that the Son of God had to become human and die on a cross for us. We are confident that he hears us and he will grant our prayers according to his will—even if he has to change what we pray for along the way.

John does include one qualification, however. John tells us that we can pray confidently for prodigal believers and that God will restore life to those prodigal believers, but John also specifies that he is talking about believers who are "sinning a sin not leading to death" and then again that God will grant life "to those whose sinning does not lead toward death" (verse 16). So what do these phrases mean?

Based on the context of this entire letter, the "sin leading to death" is most likely a persistent rejection of Jesus as the

Christ and the Son of God, which inevitably leads to a sinful separation from the church of faithful believers (see 1 John 3:18–27 and 4:1–6). This interpretation is debated among biblical scholars, but given the fact that John has warned multiple times in this letter that we should not follow the antichrists and false prophets who "went out from us, but... were not from us" (1 John 2:19), it seems likely that this is what John means by "a sin leading to death."

In regard to such people, John writes, "There is a sin leading toward death; I do not say that he should pray concerning this" (verse 16). John warns us that we cannot pray with the same level of confidence for those who are committing this sin that leads to death. Still, we should not read more into John than what he says here. There are two cautions about this passage that we ought to keep in mind.

First, while John enigmatically says, "There is a sin leading toward death; I do not say that he should pray concerning this," we should keep in mind that he does not forbid us from praying for those who commit the sin that leads to death. I point this out so we aren't hindered in our prayers by a concern about praying for the wrong people. God may, at some point, instruct us to stop praying for a particularly hard–hearted person, just as he told Jeremiah to stop praying for the hard–hearted Israelites, but that is his business. We should pray until God tells us not to.[2]

Second, this text is meant to lead us to confident prayer and not to obsessive speculation on what the sin leading to death might be. John's point is that praying for such a brother is the will of God ("if we ask something according to his will he hears us") and that God has made special promises to restore such wanderers through our prayers—with the warning that God will occasionally direct us not to pray for them any longer. Praying for the prodigal believer is the rule; not praying on the basis of the sin leading to death is the exception.

It is important that we keep our focus on prayer, since we frequently make praying for the restoration of wandering believers too complicated for ourselves. We hope problems will go away on their own. We worry that we might offend our friends. We justify our non-action by Jesus' warnings to avoid hypocrisy (Matthew 7:1–5). Or, we simply don't take the time to listen to the hurts, doubts, or struggles of our fellow believers.

Throughout John's entire letter he has been preaching the necessity of loving one another, and now he outlines one of the key ways we demonstrate such love: prayer. God's will (1 John 5:14) is that we would love his other children so deeply that we would not cease to pray fervently for their souls, to prevent them from further chasing after sin.

But do keep this in mind: typically, when we begin to pray for our friends in this way, God starts to call us to play a role in confronting and leading them back to Jesus. Thankfully, God works in our hearts as we pray to wipe away the pride and judgmental attitudes that Jesus condemned so that we can proclaim nothing but the gospel when we approach our friends: "I'm not worthy, and you aren't worthy, but Jesus died for us anyway. Don't make shipwreck of your faith. Don't wander into sin leading to death. Repent and believe the gospel again!"

In fact, the text of verse 16 suggests that God will use us, in and through our confident prayers, as the vessels through which he grants life to our fellow believers. There is some debate on this, but I would paraphrase verse 16 this way: "If someone sees his brother sinning a sin not leading to death, he [the one who sees his brother] shall ask, and he [God] will give him [the one who sees his brother] life *for the sake* of those who sin the sins that do not lead to death."

The second "him" ("...and God will give him") and the phrase "to those whose sinning does not lead toward death" are probably not referring to the same person, because the former is singular and the latter is plural. Greek doesn't necessarily always follow that rule, but the grammar here is strong evidence for the interpretation I am outlining. God gives one person (singular) life, and he gives it on behalf of those (plural) who commit sins that do not lead to death. The best explanation is that God intends us to pray confidently because he plans on using us as the vessels of conveying life to prodigal believers. R. C. H. Lenski writes:

> Here is a brother that is living in some sin (present, durative participle), and one of us (singular) sees it. Knowing what we all know about asking God and about God's hearing us, one of us asks God, and God gives this one life for this brother, "for those sinning"; the plural indicates that there will be others that sin from time to time.... What God does when he gives life for these sinners is to strengthen their damaged, declining spiritual life, which they have not as yet lost.[3]

God is calling us to deep love for our neighbor that will not only commit to fervent prayer for their holiness but that will result in being the means through which God restores life to them. What a privilege to minister to one another in this way—God actually uses us, through our confident prayers, to restore and heal one another!

But remember, this great privilege of prayer is built on our confidence, and our confidence is built on our assurance of eternal life, which we find in Jesus Christ, the Son of God. The one who has the Son has life, and everyone who has eternal life in the Son ought to demonstrate their confidence through prayer—especially prayer for prodigal believers.

QUESTIONS FOR REFLECTION

1. Has your understanding of what discipleship training should look like changed at all through studying 1 John? If so, how?
2. In what ways has 1 John helped you to know that you have eternal life?
3. When you feel confident, are you inclined to pray more or less? How does John's definition change how we normally think about confidence?
4. Who are the prodigal believers whom you need to pray for?

11
Eternal Life

1 John 5:18–21

As we have talked about, 1 John is not written as a straight, linear argument that builds one topic upon another, always moving forward and progressing through the material. The Apostle Paul writes that way, but not John. Instead, John writes this letter in a spiral, addressing God's righteousness, our sin, our salvation, our love for one another, and then finally starting back again at the beginning. These four topics all spill into one another, so that John goes back and forth, developing and applying, reminding and clarifying, always moving closer to the center of his message.

Over the course of chapter 5, John's spiral is quickly tightening. As he arrives at the core of his purpose for writing this letter, the tone of his writing intensifies. John has written about faith, God's testimony, the life that is in the Son of God, our confidence before God, and prayer. But now, as we come to the end of 1 John, the apostle leaves us with three "we have come to know" statements and one command at the climax of his message.

PROTECTION FROM THE EVIL ONE

In 1 John 5:18, the apostle writes the first of these statements:

> We have come to know that everyone who has been

born of God does not practice sin, but *he* who was born of God protects [lit. "keeps"] him, and the evil *one* does not touch him.

Just as he did in 1 John 3:4–10, John here explains that being born of God is incompatible with continuing, ongoing sin. And, just as in 1 John 3:4–10, John is not saying that "real" Christians are somehow sinless. John knows full well that all believers sin, and he made this abundantly clear in the opening of this letter when he wrote that anyone who claims to be without sin is a liar (1 John 1:6, 8, 10). Additionally, recall that John revealed only a few verses earlier in 1 John 5:13 his purpose for writing this letter: so that we may know that we have eternal life.

So, when John writes that "everyone who has been born of God does not practice sin," he is not casting doubt on the genuineness of our salvation. Instead, he has two senses of meaning in mind: (1) a description of the new nature of those born of God; and (2) an exhortation to continue to put the remaining sin in our lives to death by the grace of Christ.

First, John genuinely wants to convey that we have been radically transformed by being born of God so that we cannot sin any longer without remorse. When we become the children of God, we slowly begin to lose our appetite for the sin we once enjoyed—and even when we do give into temptation, we do not gain the satisfaction from sin that we once did. Instead, God's Spirit convicts us of our sin and leads us to repent (turn) from what we have done back to God, seeking forgiveness through the gospel. It isn't that sin is impossible but rather that ongoing sin is unsustainable in the life of someone who has been born of God.

Second, John writes this statement to urge us to abandon whatever sin still remains in our lives. Although this isn't phrased as a command, we need to read this as John's gentle but firm nudge toward holy living. It is as though John is saying, "If we have come to know that everyone who has been born of God does not keep on sinning, then shouldn't you put to death whatever sin still entangles you?"

We are not alone, however, in waging war against the lingering sin in our lives. On the contrary, John is explicit that we have supernatural help, for "he who was born of God protects" us. This is a play on words, moving from describing "everyone who has been born of God" (i.e., all believers) to then singling out the one person who could be described as "he who was born of God"—that is, the only begotten Son of God, Jesus.

Jesus is our Great Protector not only against sin but even against the evil one himself. No matter what temptation the Great Tempter throws at us—despair, lust, envy, greed, pride, hatred, and so on—John tells us that Satan cannot "touch" (which we might translate as "fasten to, take hold of, cling to") us because of the perfect protection of the Son of God.[1] When Jesus died on the cross, he purchased not only our forgiveness from sin but also the grace that enables us to live holy lives. When we are armed with this grace, Satan is simply not in an evenly matched fight. It is not as though God passively watches us from heaven, curious to see how well we end up doing. The whole story of the gospel is that God actively came down from heaven to come to our rescue!

So, as you struggle against your sin, remember that God himself has sworn an unbreakable oath to assist you—the Father issued the promise, the Son sealed the promise in his own blood, and the Spirit confirms the promise by his anointing on your life. He who was born of God protects you, even at the cost of his own life. And if God himself is for you, then the evil one has no power to touch you.

THE WHOLE WORLD LIES IN THE EVIL ONE

In the second "we have come to know" statement with which he closes his first letter, John writes:

> We have come to know that we are of God, and the whole world lies in the evil one. (1 John 5:19)

Here, John writes that we who look to Jesus Christ for salvation may have absolute confidence in our origin, which is that we are of God (*ek tou theou*), a shortened form of saying that we have been born of God (*ho gegennemenos ek tou theou*, as in 1 John 5:18). And if we know that we have been born of God, we may be confident that God has indeed given us eternal life. In other words, if we are confident about our new birth, we may be confident as we go to our death.

But just as glorious as the gospel of Jesus Christ is for the believer, the curse of the evil one is equally terrifying for the unbeliever. John writes literally that "the whole world lies in the evil one," but the ESV translators added "in the power of" to make more sense of the phrase. John's image portrays the world as entirely powerless under the dominion of the evil one.

Perhaps most tragically, the world thinks that they are the ones who are really living. They do anything and everything they please, and they imagine that in chasing after every opportunity available to them, they have life. But it is in doing those very things that they actually enslave themselves more and more to Satan.

There are only two kingdoms in this world: the kingdom of the evil one and the kingdom of our God and of his Christ. Every human being is a subject of one of these kingdoms, without exception. The kingdom of the evil one is death and slavery; the kingdom of the Lord Jesus Christ is life and freedom.

But John Stott draws our attention to an important point concerning John's describing the lost as the "whole world": "We need to remember, however, that although the whole world lies in the power of the evil one, it is for the sins of the whole world (the only other occurrence of the expression in the Epistle) that Jesus Christ is the propitiation (ii. 2)."[2] The gospel holds out hope to the lost—even to those whom we might consider the most lost in their subjection to the kingdom of the evil one. The gospel gives this command:

believe in the Lord Jesus Christ and you will be saved from the dominion of darkness, being transferred into the kingdom of God's beloved Son, in whom we have redemption, the forgiveness of sins.

JESUS IS THE TRUE GOD AND ETERNAL LIFE

The third "we have come to know" statement as John closes his first letter is one of the most precious verses to me in the entire Bible:

> But we have come to know that the Son of God came and he has given to us understanding so that we may know the True One, and we are in the True One, in his Son Jesus Christ. This one is true God and eternal life. (1 John 5:20)

Once again, John loads his deceptively simple sentences with massive theological freight. Here, John is highlighting three facets of Jesus' glory: first, the objective and subjective knowledge that Jesus has given to us; second, the personal knowledge of God the Father that Jesus has invited us into; and third, the direct experience of God that we have in Jesus.

OBJECTIVE AND SUBJECTIVE KNOWLEDGE OF JESUS

First, John emphasizes both the objective and the subjective knowledge of Jesus, the Son of God. Objectively, Jesus the Son of God "has come." Though he is the Word who was in the beginning with God and who was himself God, he humbly took on the nature of humanity also, being born to a virgin in Bethlehem. This God–man lived a perfect life and then gave up his life on a Roman cross at the demand of his fellow Jewish people. On the third day, he rose again from the dead.

This actually happened in real history. It is not merely something I feel or wish. Jesus was born, Jesus died, and Jesus rose again. We can build our faith with confidence upon the solid foundation of these historical facts.

There is, however, another critical component to the objective knowledge that we have of Jesus. Even more than relating the merely human history of Jesus, the Scriptures also testify that God was at work doing something cosmically significant in and through the life, death, and resurrection of Jesus: "in Christ God was reconciling the world to himself" (2 Corinthians 5:19). Part of our objective knowledge about Jesus revolves around what God reveals to us in the Bible by pulling back the curtain and letting us peek into the throne room of heaven to hear God's own eternal decrees.

Look at it another way: on the surface, it isn't terribly interesting to learn that the Romans executed Jesus on the cross. To put the crucifixion of Jesus into perspective, consider that the Roman general Crassus once crucified six thousand people at the same time after he defeated them in battle.[3] From a purely human perspective, Jesus' death was not unique at all, but from God's perspective, Jesus' death is the power of God unto salvation. None of those six thousand people (nor anyone else, for that matter) died as a substitutionary sacrifice for the human race. The objective facts about Jesus are historical, but they are also supernatural.

After John emphasizes the objective aspects of Christ's ministry, he also reminds us that God has made known to us the extraordinary things he accomplished through Jesus. Subjectively, Jesus has "given us understanding." Not only have we been made aware of the story of Jesus, but also Jesus has opened our eyes to see, our ears to hear, our hearts to believe, and our minds to understand the significance of the story. The life, death, and resurrection of Jesus is more than an impersonal history lesson to us, but by the Holy Spirit, God has made this gospel to be our only hope in this life and the next.

It is critical that the message of Jesus the Son of God should be both objective fact and subjective experience. Otherwise, the gospel simply is not good news. If the gospel is not objectively true—so that the Son of God did not become human for us and for our salvation as the Scriptures say he did—then all the emotional satisfaction in the world wouldn't make a difference. As Paul writes to the Corinthians, "If in Christ we have hope in this life only, we are of all people most to be pitied" (1 Corinthians 15:19). But by the same token, if this message had never reached our ears or never penetrated our hearts, then the message would never become good news for us. John never wants us to forget the lavish grace God has demonstrated toward us in the way he subjectively opened our eyes to the objective goodness of the gospel.

PERSONAL KNOWLEDGE OF GOD THROUGH JESUS

Second, the purpose of both Jesus' coming and his giving us understanding is "so that we may know the True One." Just as we saw in the first verses of 1 John, truth is a person. John's goal is that we may know the True One.

To know the True One in this way would mean far more than simply being aware of him. For example, I am aware that George Washington was the first president of the United States and I am aware of a few details surrounding his life, but we never had a conversation together and he never even knew my name. John means something far more than mere awareness when he talks about the way we know God.

The knowledge John is talking about is intimate, even beyond the intimacy I share with my closest friends or even my wife, since God knows me in a way that no other human possibly could. God created me, so he understands the depths of my deepest doubts, joys, fears, loves, pains, and satisfactions, even before I am aware of them myself.

But this knowledge runs in two directions. Not only does God know us, but God has also allowed us to know him. Paul writes about the mystery of our knowledge of God in 1 Corinthians 2. He explains:

⁹But, as it is written,
"What no eye has seen, nor ear heard,
    nor the heart of man imagined,
what God has prepared for those who love him"—

¹⁰these things God has revealed to us through the Spirit. For the Spirit searches everything, even the depths of God. ¹¹For who knows a person's thoughts except the spirit of that person, which is in him? So also no one comprehends the thoughts of God except the Spirit of God. ¹²Now we have received not the spirit of the world, but the Spirit who is from God, that we might understand the things freely given us by God. (1 Corinthians 2:9–12)

The Spirit of God searches the depths of God, and God has given us of his Spirit so that we might understand the things freely given us by God—that is, so that we could know God the Father intimately by the Spirit, through Christ.

Jesus came so that we may enjoy an intimate, personal knowledge of the True One, God the Father. This knowledge of God the Father is personal and relational, and the joy of this kind of knowing God is eternal life itself (see John 17:3). The Son of God came and gave us understanding so that we may know the True One.

DIRECT EXPERIENCE OF GOD IN JESUS

Third, John writes that our experience of God runs far deeper than knowledge, even deeper than the kind of intimate, relational knowledge we just discussed. More than knowledge, John now explains that, in Jesus, we have a direct experience of God: "we are in the True One, in his Son Jesus Christ. This one is true God and eternal life."

The stunning thing about this statement is that John speaks of Jesus not as our way of coming to the Father but as the "True One." The "in" statements seem to point to the same person: "in the True One" refers to "in his Son Jesus Christ."

Therefore, when John writes the climax of the entire book, "This one is true God and eternal life," he is still referring to Jesus the Son, who is himself true God and eternal life. The word translated "he" has the sense of "this one," which would refer to the previous phrase: "and we are in the True One, in his Son Jesus Christ."

Jesus is true God and eternal life.

R. C. H. Lenski describes the glorious way John slowly reveals more, bit by bit, before this stunning declaration that Jesus is himself true God and eternal life:

> So John has hitherto called Jesus "the Son of God" and "his (the Father's, God's) Son," and now, here at the end and the climax, John duplicates and calls also Jesus Christ the real God's Son because he is the real God's only begotten Son (4:9), yea, "the real God." As the Father is the real (genuine) God, so his Son is the real (genuine) God, and this Son places us in fellowship with the Father. Need we add the words that Jesus himself spoke in John 10:30; 12:45; 14:9?[4]

Because Jesus is himself true God and eternal life, all the riches of the triune God are ours if we are in Christ— the abiding presence of the Holy Spirit, the pleasures of fellowship with the Father, and the glorious eternal life of the Son of God.

This is the unspeakably magnificent gospel of Jesus Christ, God's Son, who is himself true God and eternal life. Our only fitting response to this revelation is to worship Jesus with all our heart, soul, mind, and strength.

LITTLE CHILDREN, KEEP YOURSELVES FROM IDOLS

The last verse of John's letter has puzzled commentators for centuries:

> Little children, keep yourselves from idols. (1 John 5:21)

John has not mentioned the word *idol* once throughout his entire letter, so why would he end so abruptly with this command? Let's look a little closer at the topic of idolatry.

Certainly, John does not address formal idolatry up to this point. John nowhere discusses the making of idols nor sacrificing to them nor eating the meat sacrificed to them nor the cultic prostitution that was so prevalent in idol worship nor even the human sacrifice that many false gods supposedly demanded. These issues are confronted elsewhere in the Bible, but not here.

On another level, however, we might say that John has written about nothing other than idolatry if we define idolatry as anything that distracts us from worshiping Jesus Christ, who is the true God and Eternal Life himself. Whenever we entertain false ideas about the true God or offer false obedience to God's commandments, then we are guilty of the sin of idolatry. And if John is looking at idolatry as this kind of general idea that encompasses all kinds of things that would distract us from Christ, then this is the perfect place for John to end his letter. This verse is the definitive, all–inclusive word of application after a long sermon, bringing everything into real-life perspective.

So, let's begin to apply John's application to our own lives. Which things are distracting us from Christ? Sometimes we pursue specific sins God has forbidden in his law, whether to lie or to steal or to covet or to commit adultery. When we pursue these sins, we actually begin to worship them in some sense by seeking our ultimate joy and satisfaction in them, rather than in Jesus. That's idolatry in a nutshell.

But we can also commit idolatry with legitimate relationships and activities in our lives, such as in our jobs, spouses, children, friends, or hobbies. These things become idols when they consume our lives to an unhealthy degree. Whenever you elevate even good things to a place beyond the one God has intended them to occupy in your life, those good things become the idols you worship.

Regardless of your specific idolatry, it is incredibly important that we don't isolate this single verse as John's description of how we defeat sin in our lives. John is pleading with us to avoid sin, but he isn't suggesting that the way to conquer idolatry is just to try really, really hard to "keep yourselves from idols." Yes, those are the words John uses, but this verse isn't all he has said. All the rest of of 1 John concerns itself with the glory of Christ in his gospel; only in this one last verse does John tell us to keep ourselves from idols.

The way to conquer sin is to take into account everything else John has written up to this point by seeking to love Christ more than your idols. When sinful temptations arise in our hearts, we must preach to ourselves that the genuine longing of our hearts is to have Christ, not the temptation. When legitimate relationships and activities seek to crowd out Christ, we must preach to ourselves that we will lose whatever we put above Christ; only when we seek the kingdom of God first does God add to us all these other things. The gospel is always the best weapon when we fight against temptation.

And so, little children, keep yourselves from idols.

1. How have you experienced unsustainable sin in your life? That is, where have you seen God's grace keeping you from pursuing sin as completely or as fully as you might have done before you came to know Jesus?

2. Which do you tend to value more: the objective knowledge of Jesus (historical facts and supernatural significance) or your subjective experience of Jesus (the work of the Holy Spirit in making the gospel real to you)? Why do you think that is? Why is the other kind of knowledge of Jesus so important, and what would it look like to balance out the two in your mind?

3. What idols do you have in your life? What illegitimate things are you pursuing? What legitimate things have become so important that they are distracting you from Jesus himself?

4. What would be the first three things that would change in your life if you genuinely loved Jesus more than anyone or anything else?

12
The Case Study of the Elect Lady

2 John

The book of 1 John does not exhaust everything John has to teach us about Christian discipleship. The letter certainly functions as a foundational handbook for learning Christian discipleship—as we have seen so far in our study—but John also wrote two additional letters called 2 John and 3 John that build on what he wrote in 1 John.

To understand how 2 and 3 John fit together with 1 John, it is helpful to think of them as case studies where John's discipleship training is put into practice. So, in 1 John, the apostle had written a general letter without any specific context, making it easily shared among a broad variety of Christians—even those of us who are living two thousand years after he wrote it. But in 2 and 3 John, we will now see John writing to specific groups of people who lived in specific places and who faced specific challenges in ministry and life. This specificity doesn't mean that 2 and 3 John are irrelevant to those of us living in different contexts—in fact, it is quite the opposite. Instead, 2 and 3 John provide real, concrete situations to help us understand what it looks like to follow Jesus in the midst of theological controversies (2 John) and personality conflicts (3 John).

So now, as we study these letters together, may God give us eyes to see, ears to hear, and hearts to understand all that is contained in the gospel of Jesus Christ.

LOVING ONE ANOTHER IN TRUTH

One unique aspect of 1 John is that it does not include the typical kind of greeting we find in other New Testament letters. In fact, 1 John is the only letter in the New Testament that does not contain any kind of greeting at all to the original recipients of the letter.[1] Instead, John had opened his first letter with a preface in which he immediately began bearing witness to Jesus Christ, the word of life who had been manifested in their midst.

But now in 2 John—and again in 3 John—John does write a more formal, typical greeting that sounds much more like what we find in the other New Testament letters. He identifies himself as "the elder," and he names the recipients of his letter as a group of people he calls "the elect lady and her children":

> [1]The elder to the elect lady and to her children, whom I love in truth, and not I only but also all those who have come to know the truth, [2]because the truth *is* abiding in us and will be with us forever. [3]Grace, mercy, *and* peace will be with us from God the Father and from Jesus Christ the Son of the Father, in truth and love. (2 John 1:1–3)

THE IDENTITY OF THE ELECT LADY

So, who is this "elect lady," and who are her children (2 John 1:1)? While it is possible that the "elect lady" refers to a single person so that "her children" are this woman's biological children, there are a few reasons for thinking that the "elect lady" is in fact a church and that the "children" are the members of the church.

First, John frequently used this word for "children" (*teknia*) in 1 John to refer to his own spiritual children (1 John 2:1, 28;

142

3:7, 18; 4:4; 5:21). John's normal use of the word *teknia* is to refer to spiritual children, not biological children.

Second, it would be difficult to understand the children in 2 John 1:13 as referring to biological nieces and nephews: "The children of your elect sister greet you." Why only the children? Wouldn't the "elect sister" also send her greetings if these two women were biological sisters? It seems easier to understand this as an extended metaphor to describe the members of two churches rather than the members of two related families.

Third, throughout the Old Testament, and even in the New Testament, the people of God are referred to as a woman, whether as a wife, bride, mother, or daughter or simply as "she."[2] In the context of the rest of the Bible, it is natural to read the "elect lady" as a reference to a church.

THE TRUTH
OF THE LOVE OF JESUS CHRIST,
THE SON OF THE FATHER

In 2 John 1:3, John closes out the opening section of his letter by offering a benediction where he defines the essence of the truth in terms of love. In this blessing, he writes that "Grace, mercy, and peace will be with us from God the Father and from Jesus Christ the Son of the Father, in truth and love" (2 John 1:3). This sounds virtually identical to any of the introductory benedictions from the other letters in the Scriptures by Paul or Peter, but there are five unique features in what John says here that make this particular greeting stand out.[3] After we survey these features, we'll explore why John writes such a distinctive greeting in verse 3.

First, other New Testament greetings are written as expressions of a wish or a desire, but here John uses a confident future tense. For example, Paul and Peter typically do not use any verb at all, writing their greetings to sound something like this: "Grace to you and peace from God our Father and the Lord Jesus Christ" (Romans 1:7). But in 2 John 1:3, the apostle uses the future tense to convey the certainty of his statement: "Grace, mercy, and peace *will* be with us." This is more than a desire—it's an announcement of a fact.

Second, between the words *grace* and *peace,* John adds the word *mercy,* a word we find only in the greetings that Paul writes in 1 and 2 Timothy. *Mercy* describes the reality that God has not treated us as we deserved to be treated because of our sins (i.e., badly), while *grace* describes God's unmerited favor toward us (i.e., he treats us well). *Peace* refers to our new status as those who have received both grace and mercy, cleansed from all sin and unrighteousness by the blood of Jesus (1 John 1:7, 9) and made recipients of eternal life through the witness of the Holy Spirit, who gives us Jesus Christ (1 John 5:6–12).

Third, John adds the words "the Son of the Father," affirming the trinitarian theology he wrote about in 1 John 2:18–28, where he asserted that anyone who denies that Jesus is the Son of the Father is the antichrist. Fourth, John adds the phrase "in truth and love," which (as we shall see) are the two theme virtues of 2 John. No other New Testament greeting contains the phrase "the Son of the Father" or the phrase "in truth and love."

Fifth, this is the only greeting in the entire New Testament that specifically states that the grace, mercy, and peace (or any combination of such divine blessings) come from God the Father and *from* Jesus Christ. Very often Jesus Christ is also named, but it will sound something like this: "Grace to you and peace from God our Father and the Lord Jesus Christ" (Romans 1:7), without using another word for "from" to name Jesus explicitly as the source of grace and peace. In other places, only the Father is named as the source of blessing: "Grace to you and peace from God our Father" (Colossians 1:2).

This last change from the standard New Testament greeting is very interesting, and it gives us insight into the overall reason that John has so carefully written his greeting. John is emphatic that we recognize Jesus Christ as the source of these divine gifts and graces because that means that Jesus is equal with his Father as the origin of all blessings. This is implied in the other New Testament greetings, so we shouldn't think the theology of the other letters is somehow deficient; however, only John goes out of his way to specify that grace, mercy, and peace come from the Father and from Jesus Christ the Son of the Father.

What's behind all this for John? R. C. H. Lenski explains:

> But there is a point in the repetition of [the word *from*] and in the naming of the two Givers: "from God (the) Father and from Jesus Christ, the Son of the Father." These two are equal.... John purposely repeats "the Father" in order to convey fully what he means by Jesus Christ's being "the Son" of the Father. The antichristian heresy of the deceivers made Jesus the physical son of Joseph.[4]

Against the heretics that denied the full authority of Jesus by making him inferior to the Father as the son of someone else, John announces the supremacy of Christ: Jesus is equal with the Father because he is the Son of the Father. Jesus is the fountainhead from whom all blessings flow, and Jesus is the one through whom we will receive grace, mercy, and peace—in the truth of Jesus and from the love of Jesus.

As we will see clearly in 2 John 1:7–11, the apostle writes this letter largely because he has identified dangerous, false teaching and he wants to warn the children of the elect lady against it. The false teachers refused to acknowledge the full glory of Jesus (2 John 1:7, 9), but John insists that we experience no blessing whatsoever apart from the full, unadulterated truth of Jesus Christ.

THE COMMONALITY OF TRUTH AND LOVE

But let's take a step back to see the bigger picture of what John has packed into three short verses. In the greetings of 2 John 1:1–3, the apostle is laying the foundation for the theme he wants to discuss in this letter: the tight connection between truth and love.[5] He insists that he loves the elect lady in truth and that all who know the truth also love the elect lady. Why? Because truth unites people eternally: "the truth is abiding in us and will be with us forever" (2 John 1:2). Truth is the commonality in which God's people enjoy mutual love and fellowship together. Then, in his benediction, John writes that the blessings of God come to us in truth (i.e., the truth that Jesus is the eternal Son of the Father) and love (i.e., the grace, mercy, and peace of Jesus).

We shouldn't think truth and love are new subjects to which John is introducing us in 2 John because John discussed both of these topics thoroughly in 1 John. Recall the fact that truth was the very first subject in 1 John 1:1–4 and that John continued urging us to know the truth throughout his letter (1 John 1:1–4; 2:18–27; 4:1–6; 5:1–12, 20). Additionally, John insisted on the necessity of loving one another over and over in 1 John (1 John 2:7–11, 3:11–24, 4:7–21, 5:16–17).

But while it is very clear that John wrote about truth and love in 1 John, it is also the case that John never actually clarified in his first letter *how* truth and love fit together. He simply insisted that both are necessary, and he spent his time teaching about truth and love individually.

Here in 2 John, however, the apostle reveals to us that love and truth are deeply connected. Everyone who has come to know the truth is drawn to mutual love for one another, and their mutual love is shaped and defined by the truth. Certainly, love and truth are very different from each other, but they balance, rather than cancel, each other out. You cannot separate them, and if you try to cling to only one while excluding the other, you will end up losing both.

Of course, this is a bit surprising. Truth, on the one hand, is an immovable object. We can't bargain with truth, manipulate truth, or compromise with truth, because the moment we alter truth in the least, it ceases to qualify as truth. Truth is absolute, unbendable, unchangeable, and fixed—we can take it or leave it, but the one thing we can't do is change it.

Love, on the other hand, is an unstoppable force. Love characteristically overlooks flaws and shortcomings. Love doesn't say, "Take it or leave it," but rather, "Whatever it takes." Love refuses to walk away, choosing instead to pursue, woo, and overcome any barriers whatsoever that stand in the way of reconciliation.

In 2 John, the apostle unfolds for us how each virtue needs the other. Love must temper truth, and truth must strengthen love.

IN JESUS, LOVE WINS

But doesn't there come a point where either truth or love has to give? When push comes to shove, which wins out? Should truth remain fixed and immovable, or should love's unstoppable force prevail? At the end of the day, to which virtue does God give a higher priority? And to which side should we err when we are forced to choose between the two?

John begins to answer this question by affirming the necessity of love. Here is what John writes in 2 John 1:4–6:

> [4]I rejoiced greatly that I have found *some* of your children walking in truth, just as we received the commandment from the Father. [5]And now I ask, Lady, not as a new command I am writing to you but *one* which we have had from the beginning, that we should love one another. [6]And this is the love, that we should walk according to his commandments. This is the commandment, just as you have heard from the beginning, that in this you should walk. (2 John 1:4–6)

In verse 4, John defines "walking in truth" as obedience to "the commandment from the Father." Then, in verse 5, John explicitly names the commandment that he is talking about: "not as a new command I am writing to you but one which we have had from the beginning, that we should love one another." Just as he did in 1 John 2:7, John identifies love as the commandment that we have had from the beginning, but here he also explains that obedience to this commandment to love is the definition of what it means to walk in truth. We cannot walk in truth unless we obey God's commandment to love one another.

What this means is that truth isn't purely an intellectual exercise, where your only job is to get your facts straight. Instead, real truth fuels warmth, affection, and deep concern for your brothers and sisters in the truth. As a perfect example of this principle, John describes how he himself rejoices in love for his fellow believers when he sees some of the lady's children walking in truth. His passion for seeing other people walk in truth creates his deep love for them.

Seeing this connection between truth and love helps us immensely to understand the nature of the gospel. As we talked about in the very first chapter of this book, truth is a person, not some vague knowledge that stays aloof from us, hidden in some far corner of the universe. Truth himself—the person of Jesus Christ—was not willing to remain distant from us in the heaven of heavens, passively waiting for someone righteous enough to earn entry into his presence. Rather, his own love compelled him to pursue his people no matter what it would cost him.

In Jesus, love *does* win.

But in Jesus, truth wins too.

IN JESUS, TRUTH WINS TOO

For John, love cannot be the complete, final word, because truth *always* balances out love. When serious threats arise contrary to the truth of Jesus Christ, truth compels love to face those problems directly. For this reason, John concludes his short letter with a strict warning:

> [7]For many deceivers have gone out into the world, those who do not confess Jesus Christ having come in the flesh. This one is the deceiver and the antichrist. [8]Watch yourselves, that you may not lose what we have worked for but that you may receive a full reward.

[9]Everyone *who* goes ahead and does not remain in the teaching of Christ does not have God. The one *who* abides in the teaching, this one has both the Father and the Son. [10]If someone comes to you and does not bring that teaching, do not receive him into your house and do not speak a greeting to him. [11]For the one *who* speaks a greeting to him has fellowship in his wicked works.

[12]Having many things to write to you, I do not wish *to write* through paper and ink, but I hope to come to you and to speak face-to-face, that our joy may be filled up. [13]The children of your elect sister greet you. (2 John 1:7–13)

The background behind what John writes here is that, in his day, Christian missionaries would move from city to city, receiving food and lodging from other Christians living in the city where they were doing ministry. This network of hospitality was critical for providing the basic needs of the missionaries who were among the first to announce the gospel of Jesus to the wider world, but there were several challenges with this system. John Stott helpfully explains that these problems were the motivation for John to write 2 and 3 John:

> Such hospitality [toward traveling missionaries] was open to easy abuse, however. There was the false teacher, on the one hand, who yet posed as a Christian: should hospitality be extended to him? And there was the more obvious mountebank, the false prophet with false credentials, who was dominated less by the creed he had to offer than by the material profit and free board and lodging that he hoped to gain. It is against this background that we must read the Second and Third Epistles of John, for in them the Elder issues instructions concerning whom to welcome and whom to refuse, and why.[6]

It is not love, John explains, to welcome false teachers into your midst. Love craves boundaries, adamant about preventing poisonous teaching from taking root in the church. So, truth teaches love how to recognize the ways false teaching is destructive, harmful, and deadly.

Practically, truth also warns love against extending hospitality too quickly to anyone who might bring such dangers into the church. In fact, truth refuses to let us even "speak a greeting" to a false teacher, because to do so could imply some level of commonality with that false teacher— and therefore, with their false teaching—which would be tantamount to "fellowship in his wicked works" (2 John 1:10–11). Truth guides love to recognize that even something as innocent as a greeting to such a false teacher would be confusing and destructive to the children of God who might not be capable of differentiating truth from error yet.

We should notice, however, that John does not focus his opposition against the victims of this false teaching (those who have been deceived by false teachers) but rather toward those who do the deceiving. As Christians, we are called to deal gently with those who are in error, in the hopes that they may eventually be saved. For example, Paul writes this admonition to Timothy:

> [24]And the Lord's servant must not be quarrelsome but kind to everyone, able to teach, patiently enduring evil, [25]correcting his opponents with gentleness. God may perhaps grant them repentance leading to a knowledge of the truth, [26]and they may come to their senses and escape from the snare of the devil, after being captured by him to do his will. (2 Timothy 2:24–26)

There are many who are deceived, and if we ignored everyone who did not already have a perfect understanding of the truth, no one would ever hear the saving message of Jesus Christ. With those who do not know Jesus, we should be patient and kind, praying that God will grant them repentance that leads to a knowledge of the truth. In 2 John, the apostle is singling out the false *teachers,* not those who are falsely *taught*, as deceivers and antichrists, unworthy of our greetings.

But at the same time, we cannot minimize the fact that anyone who embraces false teaching faces severe consequences as well. John pleads with this church: "Watch yourselves, that you may not lose what we have worked for but that you may receive a full reward" (2 John 1:8). Then, he clearly states the full implications of what is at stake here: "Everyone who goes ahead and does not remain in the teaching of Christ does not have God" (2 John 1:9). John does not fight for the truth in this congregation because he enjoys fighting; he fights for the truth because no one can "have God" apart from the truth of Jesus Christ. Out of deep love for this church, John contends for the full truth in their midst.

Quite simply, the truth that Jesus Christ has come in the flesh is not a debatable issue. Instead, the truth of Jesus Christ is life itself. As John wrote in 1 John 5:12, "The one who has the Son has the life; the one who does not have the Son of God does not have life." Jesus Christ's coming in the flesh is the only message that gives life to broken, needy sinners like us.

Those who love this truth have eternal life because everyone who has the Son (who himself is truth) has life. Those who reject this truth (i.e., those who reject the Son who came in the flesh) are left only with death because everyone who does not have the Son of God does not have life. There is no third option, and John is calling us to choose life, that we might live.

Truth teaches love that real, genuine care and compassion are impossible if we tolerate the poison of false teaching to fester within the church. Truth shows love how to guard one another well, so that we do not lose what we have worked for and so that we all may win a full reward. Truth reminds love that our only lasting good is found in the full, robust teaching of Jesus Christ, through whom we are reconciled to the Father by the power of the Holy Spirit.

In Jesus, truth wins too.

But here's how this balancing act between truth and love works, practically speaking. On the one hand, truth gives love the courage to stand against the deceivers and antichrists who teach a form of spirituality yet deny (or simply "do not confess") the coming of Jesus Christ in the flesh. But on the other hand, love never lets truth forget the ultimate purpose behind contending for doctrine: the glory of God and the good of the flock.

Truth calls everyone to repent from sin in order to join the fellowship of those who walk in the truth. Truth insists that salvation comes only through the gospel of Jesus Christ as the eternal Son of the Father who has come in the flesh. Truth demands that we follow the straight path of God's commandment to love one another. But unfailingly, love throws the door open wide, pursuing sinners with the gospel and urging them to turn from their sin in order to gain Jesus.

If we want to know what a perfect blend of truth and love looks like, we should look to Jesus at the cross. There, Jesus went to affirm the truthfulness of God's holiness and his righteous judgment in wrath against our sin by embracing all that we deserved, dying in our place. At the cross, Jesus exalted the goodness of truth with deadly seriousness, fulfilling every last bit of the holy law of God and being crushed by the immovable object of God's truth in the process.

But at the cross, Jesus also became the unstoppable force of God's love, doing every last thing it took to purchase his people back from sin, death, and the dominion of Satan. Jesus refused to walk away from us, but he pursued us all the way to hell, tasting the full horror of death for us so that we would not.

And if in this way God loved us in truth, we also ought to love one another—in the relentless pursuit of the truth of Jesus Christ together.

QUESTIONS FOR REFLECTION

1. When you think about God, do you imagine that he prioritizes love or truth?
2. What is a specific situation in your life where your truth needs to be tamed by love, or where your love needs to be guided by truth? What would it look like to strike a balance in that situation?

13

The Case Study of Gaius and Diotrephes

3 John

I n the case study from 2 John, the apostle explored how tightly truth and love fit together. While we might have thought John had been contrasting two polar opposites throughout 1 John when he spoke about truth and love—one an immovable object and the other an unstoppable force—we learned in 2 John that each virtue guides and shapes the character of the other. You cannot have genuine truth without love, and you cannot have pure love without truth. The book of 2 John is about demonstrating unity between two critical values in our discipleship.

John's third letter, on the other hand, is a case study that was written not to teach us how seek unity but to show us how to deal with controversy. In 3 John, we see the stark contrast between two men who love different people. Gaius, the man to whom John writes this letter, loves Jesus more than anything else. He gives generous support to missionaries to help them along as they proclaim the name of Jesus to the Gentiles who haven't yet heard about him (3 John 1:5–8), and he gives generously to them despite the fact that he is not a materially prosperous man (3 John 1:2). Diotrephes, on the other hand, loves *himself* more than anything else, so that the Apostle John describes him as a "lover of putting himself first" (3 John 1:9).

In 3 John, the apostle gives us glimpses into the end result of two kinds of discipleship: in Gaius, we see the fruit of following Jesus, and in Diotrephes, we see the fruit of following after our own sinful, selfish desires. Everyone is someone's disciple, so we all face only one question: what kind of a master will we serve?

No Greater Joy

In 3 John, "the elder" John writes another letter of roughly the same length as 2 John. (Both letters could have been written on a single sheet of papyrus.)[1] In this letter we meet Gaius, a man whom the Apostle John holds in the highest esteem. John writes this in his introduction:

> [1]The elder to the beloved Gaius, whom I love in truth. [2]Beloved, concerning all things I pray *for* you to be prospered and to be in *good* health, just as your soul prospers. [3]For I rejoiced greatly when the brothers came and bore witness to your truth, just as you are walking in truth. [4]I have no greater joy than to hear *that* my little children *are* walking in truth. (3 John 1:1–4)

Elsewhere in the New Testament, there are at least two men named Gaius who are both connected with the Apostle Paul, including a Gaius of Derbe (Acts 20:4), who is probably the same Gaius as in Acts 19:29. Then, there is the Gaius whom Paul baptized in Corinth (1 Corinthians 1:14). Since many scholars believe Paul's letter to the Romans was written from Corinth, the Gaius whom Paul names as his host at the end of the letter in Romans 16:23 is probably the same man mentioned in 1 Corinthians. We do not know, however, whether any of these men is the same Gaius whom John addresses here in 3 John.[2]

What John does make clear in these opening verses, however, is that Gaius loves Jesus with everything he has, which thrills John. John illustrates his deep admiration for Gaius's spiritual maturity in three ways. First, John addresses Gaius as a man whom he "loves in truth," which is an identical phrase to what John wrote in 2 John 1:1 to describe his relationship to the elect lady and her children. This phrase describes mutual admiration and affection on the basis of a common love of the truth—a fellowship based on their shared love for the truth of Jesus.

Second, John offers a prayer of blessing for Gaius's prosperity and health. This isn't the kind of health–and–wealth prayer we tend to hear from proponents of the so–called prosperity gospel, as though John were claiming money and good health for Gaius here through "faith." In fact, the emphasis of John's prayer is not on the blessings but on Gaius's maturity. Donald Burdick makes this observation:

> The contrast between Gaius's physical and material condition, on the one hand, and his spiritual condition, on the other, was rather striking. His spiritual prosperity seems to have exceeded his material prosperity. Too often in that day, as well as this, just the reverse was true.[3]

The apostle is not offering a polite wish for prosperity and good health, and he isn't suggesting that God is obligated to reward Gaius for his godliness with money and health. Instead, John is simply praying that God would bless Gaius, a man who loves God, by matching his spiritual vitality with material prosperity and physical health.

If you think about it, that's quite a daunting prayer. Would you pray that God would adjust your physical health and your wealth to match the level of your spiritual strength?

Third, John exclaims his great joy in verse 3 upon hearing that Gaius is "walking in truth"—again, a very similar phrase to what John had written in his second letter (2 John 1:4). Apparently, John had sent to this church some of his own missionaries("the brothers," 3 John 1:3), who reported back to John that Gaius was "walking in truth." This phrase extends the idea of truth beyond memorizing a set of facts, suggesting that the truth of the gospel of Jesus Christ had permeated every aspect of Gaius's life. The full range of his daily life in his home, work, recreation, and so on was characterized and shaped by the truth of the gospel.

We shouldn't miss the fact that John describes Gaius as one of "my little children" (3 John 1:4). Their relationship is not a mere acquaintance, but the language instead suggests that John had personally shepherded Gaius at some point as an elder, perhaps leading him originally to a saving knowledge of Jesus, or at least taking some kind of direct spiritual responsibility for him at some point along the way. John's joy overflows in this passage out of deep satisfaction for seeing his ministry bear such great fruit in the life of Gaius.

This is why John writes in verse 4 that he has "no greater joy than to hear hear that my little children are walking in truth." John genuinely finds his greatest joy in seeing Jesus Christ glorified. He loves to see sinners repent from their sins, because their repentance honors Jesus. He labors to see people embrace the truth of the gospel for salvation, because their faith glorifies Jesus. He pours out his whole life in ministry toward seeing believers begin to live differently, because as they walk in newness of life, they exalt Jesus as worthy of all glory, honor, and praise. In Gaius, then, John rejoices because he sees his own life's work and ministry bearing much fruit.

MISSIONS FOR THE SAKE OF THE NAME

We cannot understand John's love for Gaius unless we understand what John taught us in 2 John: love for our fellow believers is inseparably connected to the truth of Jesus Christ. Finally, in 3 John 1:5–8, John discusses in detail what Gaius had done specifically to earn the apostle's unrestrained praise, namely, he had shown hospitality to missionaries whom John had sent to Gaius's city:

⁵Beloved, you do a faithful *thing*, whatever you do to these brothers and strangers, ⁶who testified to your love before the church, *for* whom you will do well sending *them* on their journey in a manner worthy of God. ⁷For the sake of the name they went out, receiving nothing from the Gentiles. ⁸Therefore we ought to receive *with hospitality* such as these, that we may become fellow-workers for the truth. (3 John 1:5–8)

As in 2 John, the backdrop of 3 John is the movement of Christian missionaries from city to city, preaching and teaching the gospel of Jesus, planting and strengthening churches wherever they went. Because this was not a time when restaurants were readily available or when clean and safe lodging was easy to find, missionaries depended on the support of other Christians who lived in the cities where they were ministering for a place to stay and to provide food as they traveled.

This is what Gaius had been doing. Though these missionaries were strangers, Gaius had done a "faithful thing" for them, doing whatever he could to support them and then "sending them on their journey" when they moved on by providing them with enough food and money to get to the next town and the next church. Because of Gaius's generosity, the missionaries were able to avoid asking for support from the Gentiles—that is, from unbelievers—which was important so that they would not be perceived as "peddlers of God's word," in the words of Paul (2 Corinthians 2:17). John says that in doing this, Gaius had become one of the missionaries' "fellow-workers for the truth."

So, in verse 6, John writes that Gaius has done well to send these missionaries on their journey "in a manner worthy of God." In other words, whatever Gaius had done for these missionaries, he had actually done to serve the one who ultimately was responsible for sending the missionaries: God. The principle is this: whenever we serve the people of God, we should do so as though we were serving God himself.

And in fact, that is exactly what we are doing. Whatever we do to the people of God—whether for good or for evil—we do to God himself. Jesus taught this idea when he told us he will say to the righteous at the final judgment, "Truly, I say to you, as you did it to one of the least of these my brothers, you did it to me" (Matthew 25:40), and to the wicked, "Truly, I say to you, as you did not do it to one of the least of these, you did not do it to me" (Matthew 25:45). Also, when Jesus stopped Saul in his tracks from persecuting Christians in Damascus, the Lord said, "Saul, Saul, why are you persecuting me?" (Acts 9:4).

This perspective helps us avoid slipping into a joyless, duty-bound sense of obligation when we support missionaries. John doesn't want to shame us into reluctantly sending some ministry a check out of nothing more than guilt. Instead, he wants to draw us into the larger vision of being involved in the mission of God in this world. Gaius was not someone in the bleachers, watching the game from a distance. Instead, by his involvement, he was an active member of the team staff on the sidelines. He may not have taken the field himself for this part of the game, but he personally invested in and worked for the entire team's success.

Guilt should never be the motivation driving us to do missions or to support missionaries. Instead, John reminds us of the true reason for missions: we do missions "for the sake of the name." As we talked about in chapter 10, when biblical writers speak of God's name, they are referring to his character, his reputation, and his deeds. To go out "for the sake of the name," then, means that we are working to spread the fame and renown and glory of Jesus to all those who have not yet heard. The reason for missions is the glory and honor of Jesus Christ.

John Piper puts this so well in his book *Let the Nations Be Glad*:

Missions is not the ultimate goal of the church. Worship is. Missions exists because worship doesn't. Worship is ultimate, not missions, because God is ultimate, not man. When this age is over, and the countless millions of the redeemed fall on their faces before the throne of God, missions will be no more. It is a temporary necessity, but worship abides forever....

But worship is also the fuel of missions. Passion for God in worship precedes the offer of God in preaching. You can't commend what you don't cherish. Missionaries will never call out, "Let the nations be glad!" who cannot say from the heart, "I rejoice in the Lord.... I will be glad and exult in you, I will sing praise to your name, O Most High" (Ps. 104:34; 9:2). Mission begins and ends in worship.[4]

This is the first challenge that 3 John presents to us. Do we love Jesus with everything we have, as John and Gaius did? Do we live to see all people come to love and worship and adore our Lord Jesus Christ?

If not, we do not need more shame heaped on us for our lack of commitment. Instead, we perhaps need more worship. The more we learn to love the worthiness of the name of Jesus, the more we will delight in being sent and sending others for the sake of his name.

DO NOT IMITATE THAT WHICH IS EVIL

But while Gaius models for us the fruit of a disciple who loves Jesus more than anything else, John moves on in the second half of his letter to address the selfishness of a man who loves himself more than anything else:

> [9]I wrote something to the church, but that lover of putting *himself* first among them—Diotrephes—does not receive us. [10]For this reason, when I come, I will bring up his works that he is doing, falsely accusing us with wicked words. And not content with this, neither does he receive the brothers, and he forbids those who desire to, and he casts them out of the church.

¹¹Beloved, do not imitate that which is evil, but that which is good. The one who does good is from God, but the one who does evil has not seen God. ¹²Demetrius has received testimony from all and from the truth itself. And we also bear testimony, and you know that our testimony is true. (3 John 1:9–12)

There is some debate about what John is referring to in verse 9 when he says, "I wrote something to the church...." It is possible, as R. C. H. Lenski suggests, that the "something" John wrote was the letter we know as 2 John, so that "the two letters were probably written on the same day and were sent to the same place, the second to the congregation, the third to one of the members."[5] If so, then the subject matter of 2 John suggests that Diotrephes was not only turning away John's missionaries but might also have been receiving false teachers, deceivers, and antichrists into the midst of the church (2 John 1:7–11).

Most commentators, however, think this must have been a letter of introduction to Gaius's church, asking them to receive John's missionaries with hospitality.[6] If this is the case, then that letter has been lost. Since 3 John does not address doctrinal errors, we have no reason to believe Diotrephes was involved in supporting false teachers. The only thing we know for sure from the limited information we have is that this is a man who wanted nothing more than to be first among everyone in the church.

So, we do not even know whether Diotrephes held any official standing in the church as a pastor, an elder, or a deacon. John simply tells us that Diotrephes was a "lover of putting himself first," without clarifying whether Diotrephes was usurping power or simply misusing the power he had lawfully received, although many commentators feel the description of Diotrephes most likely fits a person who probably did not have official status in the church.[7]

In any case, what is abundantly clear is that Diotrephes possessed an incredible amount of informal power. Perhaps

Diotrephes (or his father) had been a substantial financial supporter of the church; perhaps he held significant social or political power in the community; or perhaps he simply had a forceful personality that no one wanted to oppose. Whatever the case, Diotrephes brazenly turned away missionaries sent by the Apostle John himself, and he even went so far as to slander John (one of the hand–picked disciples of the Lord Jesus!) and his missionaries to discredit them by "falsely accusing us with wicked words" (3 John 1:10).

Why? Because Diotrephes cared nothing for Jesus—he only wanted to accumulate power for himself. Because John was an apostle, he was therefore a threat to the power that Diotrephes had built up within this community. So, John writes that Diotrephes "does not receive us" (3 John 1:9), which suggests something more along the lines of "does not acknowledge our authority."[8] In order to amass every last shred of power for himself, Diotrephes had no choice but to reject the authority of John.

When people reject everyone else's authority but their own, we should in many cases recognize their arrogance as a major red flag in their lives, a symptom revealing deeper sin problems. Time and time again, leaders who refuse accountability to anyone ultimately end up running off the rails in one way or another. Sometimes, their desire for complete freedom opens opportunities for sin that they are unable (or unwilling) to turn down. Other times, they refuse accountability because they already have something to hide. Either way, refusing to acknowledge the authority of others is not a sign of strong leadership but an early warning sign that can help alert us to the fact that we are dealing with someone who is a "lover of putting himself first."

By contrast, John's authority as an apostle is rooted not in pride or egotism but in his submission to the authority of Jesus Christ. Someone with genuine authority within the church recognizes himself first of all to be under someone else's authority.

Even Jesus considered himself to be a man under authority. When the Roman centurion asked Jesus to heal his servant, Jesus offered to go with him to heal the servant, but the centurion refused, saying, "Lord, I am not worthy to have you come under my roof, but only say the word, and my servant will be healed. *For I too am a man under authority*, with soldiers under me" (Matthew 8:8–9). Jesus marveled at the man's faith for saying such a thing—for saying that he, like Jesus, was a man under authority.

How could the centurion say truthfully that the Son of God was a man under authority? Because Jesus' authority was rooted in his submission to the Father. Paul writes this in his letter to the Philippians:

> [5]Have this mind among yourselves, which is yours in Christ Jesus, [6]who, though he was in the form of God, did not count equality with God a thing to be grasped, [7]but *emptied himself, by taking the form of a servant*, being born in the likeness of men. [8]And being found in human form, he *humbled himself* by becoming *obedient to the point of death*, even death on a cross. [9]Therefore God has highly exalted him and bestowed on him the name that is above every name, [10]so that at the name of Jesus every knee should bow, in heaven and on earth and under the earth, [11]and every tongue confess that Jesus Christ is Lord, to the glory of God the Father. (Philippians 2:5–11)

God the Father exalted Jesus and gave him the name that is above every name because Jesus had made himself nothing, taking the form of the servant, humbling himself by becoming obedient to the point of death. Jesus' obedient submission to his Father was the grounds for his exaltation and his authority over everyone in heaven and on earth and under the earth.

So, John's authority was built upon his submission to Jesus Christ, and Jesus' authority was built upon his submission to the Father. The difference between John and Diotrephes is that Diotrephes loved to put himself first, but John loved to put Christ first—just as Christ had put his Father first.

John therefore warns Gaius, "Beloved, do not imitate that which is evil, but that which is good" (3 John 1:11). The word for "imitate" is the word from which we get our word *mimeograph;* the mimeograph machine was the predecessor of the copy machine. As Christ submitted to his own Father, even to the point of dying on the cross, we should submit to Christ rather than insisting upon putting ourselves first. In our attitude, desires, and actions, we ought to be replicas (mimeographs) of the original example of humility, Jesus Christ himself. Demetrius is here commended as an exemplar of imitating the good, since he was probably the one who had carried John's letter(s) to Gaius's church.

This imitation is critical, John explains, because "the one who does good is from God, but the one who does evil has not seen God" (3 John 1:11). If we are the children of God, then like John, Gaius, and Demetrius, we will love to put Christ first. If instead we put ourselves first, then we prove we have no knowledge of God whatsoever—in fact, we prove we have never so much as seen him.

FACE-TO-FACE FELLOWSHIP

John closes with an echo from 2 John:

> [13]I had many things to write, but I do not want to write to you through pen and ink. [14]But I hope to see you shortly, and we will speak face to face. [15]Peace to you. The friends greet you. Greet the friends by name. (3 John 1:13–15)

In 2 John 1:12, John had written something nearly identical, expressing a desire to speak face-to-face rather than writing with paper and ink. From these statements, we gain an important principle for ministry. There certainly isn't anything wrong with making use of communication technology like paper, pen, ink, email, text messaging, or something similar, but we should never forget that some kinds of ministry should be conducted face-to-face, especially in the midst of severe conflict.

Consider this: in 2 John and 3 John, the apostle had written two God-breathed letters that would be included in the canon of the New Testament, but even he recognized that there were relational needs that would not have been met simply by sending these letters through paper, pen, and ink. If that is the case, then why should we think that even our most polished emails or witty text messages are sufficient to accomplish everything necessary for ministry in the body of Christ?

Messy, painful ministry—as well as encouraging, enriching ministry—can only happen to a limited degree without having direct, face-to-face contact. But if we love one another in truth, we will confront sin and exhort one another to press on for the sake of the name, and we will go to great lengths to do it face-to-face.

Beloved, walk in the truth for the sake of the name of Jesus. Do not imitate that which is evil, but that which is good. Peace to you.

QUESTIONS FOR REFLECTION

1. What brings you the greatest joy in life? Is it the name of Jesus, or something else? What preoccupies your thoughts? What kind of disappointment brings you the most pain?
2. What role have you taken up for the sake of the name?
3. How well do you submit to authority within the church? Who do you most want to put first: Jesus or yourself?
4. What ministry needs in your life right now require face-to-face conversations?

14
Discipleship
according to John

S o, what's next? Now that we have come to the end of our
study on discipleship from the letters of John, where do
we go from here? In this last chapter, let's look first at
a brief recap of each of the sections of this book. If you have
been reading this book a chapter at a time on your own or as
a part of a Bible study, it will be helpful to review the entire
book quickly.

Then we'll pull together the various sections of the book
to see the unified, coherent message John has given us so that
we can chart a clear course forward for our discipleship. By
the grace of God, let us continue following Jesus all the days
of our lives until the day he appears, when we will be like him
because we will see him as he is.

TRUTH

In the first four verses of 1 John, the apostle lays the foundation
for Christianity: truth. To paraphrase what Paul writes, If
Christianity isn't true, then we are the most pitiful people in
the whole world (1 Corinthians 15:19).

But Christianity is true. The eternal, unshakable truth
that has existed from the beginning in a face-to-face
relationship with the Father was manifested in our midst—

and this truth is a person. The truth of Christianity is not some abstract philosophical idea but the second person of the Trinity who took on human nature in our midst, Jesus Christ. And through Jesus, we have fellowship not only with God the Father but also with one another in the church that Jesus came to save.

GOSPEL

In 1 John 1:5, John gives us a message—not a good message (not gospel), but a message that should cause sinful people like you and me to take notice: God is light, and darkness is not in him, not at all. John points our attention to the contrast between the blazing glory of God's pure light and the darkness in which we walk so that we can see that we are great sinners in need of a great Savior. John cuts through the lie of the legalists who say they are without sin, as well as the lie of the libertines who say they know God but do not keep God's commandments.

Instead, John calls us to new speech. He encourages us to confess our sins, trusting in God's promise that he will be faithful to forgive us. But how could a holy God–who–is–light (in whom there is no darkness at all!) forgive sinners? John tells us: God will forgive us because justice has already been served when Jesus shed his own blood at the cross as punishment for our sin. Today, we have an advocate who faces the Father, pleading with him on our behalf, Jesus Christ the Righteous.

That is the good news of the gospel.

GROWTH

In 1 John 2:7–11, John begins to teach us the fruit of the gospel: growth. While the gospel offers free forgiveness to the worst sinners, the gospel also demands growth in our lives. Specifically, God desires that we should grow in our love for one another. The commandment to love is not a new commandment but an old commandment from the beginning. At the same time, however, Jesus made the old commandment new by a new emphasis, a new example, and a new enabling through the power of the Holy Spirit. All of us, whether young Christians or old, are called to grow together in and through this gospel of grace.

PERSEVERANCE

John did not write 1 John because he had nothing better to do. Instead, this letter is written as an urgent message to Christians on the front lines of spiritual warfare to bring us life-saving warnings about the enemy's movements. This world has real dangers that can destroy believers, and John wants to keep us from those dangers.

So, John cautions us against loving the world or the things in the world, and he urges us to instead be filled with the love of the Father. But, John only spends three verses warning us about the world. In 1 John 2:18–27, John then warns us about dangers from within the church. Antichrists will continue spreading their message denying that Jesus is the eternal Son of the Father, and John wants to ensure that our faith is not shaken. John also writes to assure us that we will persevere through this conflict by reminding us that we have the anointing of the Holy Spirit, who teaches us all things concerning the Son of God.

HOPE

In 1 John 2:28–3:3, John insists on three truths: (1) now we are children of God; (2) we are not yet what we will be when Jesus appears, when we become like him because we will see him as he is; and (3) in the meantime, between the already and the not yet, we should purify ourselves as he is pure.

Then, in chapter 3, verses 4–10, John gives another warning: if we do not practice righteousness (i.e., purify ourselves by daily repenting from sin, believing the gospel, and seeking to obey Jesus in all we do by grace) but instead continue to practice unchecked, unrepentant, ongoing sin, then we know we are not yet children of God. Instead, John warns, that kind of lifestyle is a clear sign that we remain children of the devil.

RIGHTEOUSNESS

John continues his thought in 1 John 3:11–24 by defining the exact difference between the children of God and the children of the devil: the children of God practice righteousness by loving other children of God, while the children of the devil follow in the footsteps of Cain by hating, and even murdering, the children of God. If we resemble Cain, then we are children of the devil who do not have eternal life abiding in us.

But on the other hand, John also explains that if we resemble Jesus in the way we love one another self-sacrificially (Jesus laid down his life for his people), then that love functions as evidence that we have passed over from death to life. When our hearts condemn us, this supernatural, righteousness-love helps to reassure our hearts before God.

DISCERNMENT

After assuring us of our hope, John gives another warning in 1 John 4:1–6: we must test the spirits. All around us, supernatural forces have recruited people to serve as false prophets, spreading false messages wherever we go. Specifically, John writes, these false prophets try to cast doubt on the incarnation of Jesus. John had earlier written to warn us against the antichrists who tell us Jesus is not the eternal Son of God, and now John writes to warn us about the antichrists who tell us Jesus did not become a real human being.

John insists that the gospel is true only if Jesus was fully God and fully human—anything less, and Jesus would not be able to save humankind. Whoever denies the doctrine of the incarnation is not from God but speaks from a spirit of error.

Love

After a warning, John again urges us forward in love. In 1 John 4:7–21, John reveals that love is a theological issue by telling us first that God abides in those who confess that Jesus is the Son of God (4:15) and that God abides only in those who abide in love (4:16). Why? God's nature is love, and Jesus is by nature the Son of God. If you imagine a god who is not love, or a god whose son is not Jesus, you have created a false god in your mind.

Therefore, John urges us to believe upon Jesus and to love one another just as God has loved us. The apostle warns us that we cannot claim to love God if we do not love our fellow believers, for love is from God and everyone who loves has been born of God and knows God.

Faith

In 1 John 5:1–12, John writes explicitly about the nature of our faith. First, he explains the origin of our faith: our faith is the result of the new birth God gives us by grace. We do not believe to be born again; we believe because we have been born again. Second, John characterizes our faith: our faith is nothing less than a victory of God over all the demonic powers in this world.

Third, and most important, John reveals the foundation of our faith: we believe because of the testimony the Spirit gives us, which is life itself. And furthermore, the testimony of life that the Spirit brings is nothing less than Jesus Christ himself in all his glory. "The one who has the Son has the life," John writes, and "the one who does not have the Son of God does not have life."

PRAYER

Next, John explains in 1 John 5:13–17 that this life in Jesus gives us confidence. Specifically, we have confidence in prayer, that God will answer whatever we ask of him when we ask according to his will. And even more specifically, John tells us we should exercise our confidence in prayer for the sake of prodigals who begin to depart from the faith. We have no promises concerning those who are sinning a sin leading toward death, but John urges us to love our prodigal brothers and sisters specifically by praying for those who are not yet too far gone.

ETERNAL LIFE

Finally, John comes to the center of his message in 1 John 5:18–21. John tells us three things that we have come to know during our discipleship training, and he leaves us with a single exhortation. First, we have come to know that we cannot continue sinning if we have been born of God. Jesus, the Great Protector, ensures that the evil one cannot touch us. Second, we have come to know that even though we are of God, the whole world still lies in the power of the evil one. Finally, we have come to know that Jesus came and gave us understanding so that we may know him, for Jesus is the true God and eternal life.

Therefore, John writes, keep yourselves from idols. Do not stray into anything at all that might lead you away from Eternal Life himself, whose name is Jesus.

THE CASE STUDY OF THE ELECT LADY

In 2 John, the apostle pulls together two strands of his teaching from 1 John to show their close connection: truth and love. Neither truth nor love can stand alone, but John shows that love does whatever it takes to pursue people in truth but that truth gives immovable guidelines and boundaries to protect love against the dangers of false teachers with their poisonous doctrine. In Jesus, both love and truth win.

Through this case study, John urges us never to allow our love to grow cold or to permit any compromise of the truth. If we pursue truth as a merely intellectual exercise, we miss the warm love of Christian fellowship, but if we allow false teachers in our midst, we poison ourselves with deadly teaching.

The Case Study of Gaius and Diotrephes

In 3 John, we see the practical side of John's discipleship training through the contrast of two men. In Gaius, we see Christian discipleship come to its full fruition, and in Diotrephes, we see the rotten fruit of a man who has fully rejected Jesus and sought only to put himself first. For Gaius, this looks like a man who completely loves Jesus and who gives generously of what he has to support those who are doing missions for the sake of the name of Jesus. For Diotrephes, however, we see a man who rejects all authority in order to establish his own, usurped power.

John therefore urges us not to imitate that which is evil but to imitate that which is good. We ought to give all of who we are for the glory of Jesus, as Gaius did, and we ought to take care never to pursue our own glory, as Diotrephes did.

Discipleship according to John

So where do we go from here? Through the course of 1 John, the apostle teaches us that ongoing, lifelong discipleship means four things, whether we have only recently believed in Jesus for salvation or whether we can look back on decades of following Jesus.

KNOW GOD

First, John insists everywhere through his letter that we must make a lifelong habit of studying God—not as a student studying only enough to pass a test or as a researcher who cares only about his field because of the money it pays, but as a lover who desires to know everything she can about her beloved. Because God is infinite, we will never come to the end of everything there is to know about him. Eternity with God will not be boring repetition, but we will endlessly enjoy the inexhaustible beauty and glory of God.

In his attempt to capture the full magnitude of this beauty and glory, John opens his letter with a run-on sentence about the life that was manifested among us (1 John 1:1–3). He insists that the foundation of our faith is the fact that God is light, and darkness is not in him, not at all (1 John 1:5). John explains that the Father takes the treatment of his Son personally, so that we are not allowed to imagine a non-triune god (1 John 2:18–25). John shows that we know righteousness because God is righteous (1 John 3:7) and we know love because God is love (1 John 4:8, 16). Then, John caps his letter by teaching us that to know Jesus is to have eternal life, because Jesus is true God and eternal life (1 John 5:12, 20).

In 2 John and 3 John, this theme of knowing God in truth comes to the forefront again. In 2 John, we find that in Jesus, truth wins (2 John 1:7–11). In 3 John, we see in Gaius a real-life example of what it looks like to pursue the truth with everything we have, and in Diotrephes's twisted desire to be first (3 John 1:9), we see a warning against embracing false teachers who do not confess the coming of Jesus Christ in the flesh (2 John 1:7).

Discipleship requires us to study God so that we can learn who he is. Remember that at the beginning of this book, we talked about the fact that the most basic definition of disciple is "learner" and that the most important learning is coming to know God himself as Father, Son, and Holy Spirit.

This means we need to take every opportunity we can to

study God's word. God has revealed himself in and through his word, making it possible for us to come to know him by listening to what he has spoken. Because knowing God is both our most pressing need and our highest joy, the Bible is far more practical for us than we sometimes realize. Just as I cannot have a relationship with my wife (or, at least, not a good relationship with my wife) unless I listen to what she says, we also cannot have the kind of relationship with God that he wants for us unless we listen to what he has said.

With all the false messages the false prophets bombard us with every day (1 John 4:1), listening carefully to what God has actually told us is more important than ever. As disciples of Jesus, we need to take this calling seriously by making time daily to study God's word. One resource I have found particularly helpful to study the Bible is the Robert Murray M'Cheyne Bible Reading Plan, which was written by a Scottish pastor in the nineteenth century. The standard plan assigns you about four chapters of the Bible to read every day on four different tracks through the Bible. To begin, I would recommend reading only one or two of those tracks at a time.

To help in this, I would encourage you to sign up for a daily Bible study that I write on a passage from the plan at http://freedailybiblestudy.com. I am writing these daily meditations to help people to understand every portion of Scripture in the light of the whole story, and in the light of Jesus Christ. You can read the meditations on the blog, sign up to receive them daily by email, or subscribe to listen to the material by podcast. Every meditation will cover only one of the day's readings.

Even better, ask your friends or your small group to read the same plan as you so that you can enjoy fellowship with one another, as well as with the Father and with his Son Jesus Christ (1 John 1:3). Together, you can share insights, ask questions, and pray through what you are learning about God with one another. By helping each other know God, we love one another just as God has loved us.

REPENT FROM SIN

Second, the more we study the blazing glory of God's light, we will inevitably recognize the stark contrast of our own sin. In fact, John writes, "If we say that we do not have sin, we deceive ourselves, and the truth is not in us" (1 John 1:8). Throughout 1 John, the apostle reminds us again and again of what the clear standards of God are, and he implicitly asks us to measure ourselves against those standards. Particularly, John tells us that love is the old commandment that was from the beginning (1 John 2:7, 3:11; 2 John 1:4–6) and that we must love one another, just as God has loved us (1 John 4:7).

So, John insists that part of discipleship means we recognize where we have fallen short of God's righteous requirement of love and confess that sin to God (1 John 1:9). God does not expect perfection from us, but God does call us to a lifestyle of repentance from sin—that is, a lifestyle of turning from sin and then toward God. This is what John means when he says that "everyone hoping in him purifies himself, just as he is pure" (1 John 3:3). "Practicing righteousness" (1 John 3:7, 10) does not mean practicing perfection, but instead it means regularly turning from our sin, asking God to forgive us, and praying for God to continue giving us growth, transforming us bit by bit to be like Jesus.

Remember, it is the legalist lie to deny the presence of sin in our lives (1 John 1:6, 8, 10), and it is the libertine lie to reject our need to repent from sin (1 John 2:4). John pleads with us to swallow our pride, confess our sins, and entrust ourselves to the grace of the Lord Jesus. We cannot claim to be disciples unless we regularly repent from the ways we fall short of God's glory in sin.

BELIEVE THE GOSPEL

Third, John always links repentance from sin with the promise of the gospel. When he insists that we confess our sins in 1 John 1:9, he declares that God is both faithful and just to forgive us our sins and to cleanse us from all unrighteousness by the blood of Jesus (1 John 1:7). When he acknowledges that all of us will sin in 1 John 2:1, he reminds us that "we have an advocate toward the Father, Jesus Christ the Righteous." When he encourages us to continue purifying ourselves as God is pure, he reassures us of our current confidence and our future hope: "Beloved, now we are children of God, but it has not yet been manifested what we will be. We know that when he appears, we will be like him, for we will see him as he is" (1 John 3:2).

Then, when our hearts condemn us for our failures, John reassures us that God is greater than our hearts, because God knows both where we have been and where he is taking us (1 John 3:19–21). When we see brothers and sisters sliding into sin, John urges us to believe the gospel for them, praying that God would give life to prodigal believers (1 John 5:14–16). And to close his letter, John pleads with us that we would never, ever let the gospel of Jesus Christ slip out of our sight: "Little children, keep yourselves from idols" (1 John 5:21).

Christian discipleship isn't about good people flaunting their goodness in front of bad people with holier–than–thou self–righteousness. Christian discipleship isn't about cleaning up your own life with new resolve to "do better next time." And Christian discipleship isn't about merely admiring Jesus as nothing more than a good teacher and a high moral example.

Christian discipleship is about broken, sinful, needy people openly acknowledging their inability to do anything good on their own but looking to Jesus by faith to forgive us our sins, to cleanse us from all righteousness, and to purify us as he is pure. Christian discipleship is about believing the gospel that one day Jesus will return and that when he appears we will be made like him, because we will see him as he is.

Brothers and sisters, believe the gospel. The gospel is Christianity 101, but we do not ever graduate to move beyond the gospel on to something else. The good news that Jesus Christ came into the world to destroy the works of the devil and to save sinners should never cease to humble us, convict us of our sin, lead us to repentance, draw us again to faith in Christ, and deepen our love for God the Father, God the Son, and God the Holy Spirit.

As you study God daily, and whenever you come to recognize sin in your life, turn again and again and again and again to the hope you have in Christ, because Jesus is true God and eternal life. The one who has the Son has life through the gospel.

LOVE ONE ANOTHER

Finally, John refuses to let us forget about God's commandment that we should love one another (1 John 2:7–11, 3:11, 3:23–24, 4:21, 5:2–3; 2 John 1:4–6). The gospel declares we are saved by faith alone, in Christ alone, through grace alone, but John also reminds us that saving faith is never alone. No one can fully counterfeit the kind of faith that has overcome the world because real, genuine, truth faith comes only from being born of God (1 John 5:4). And if we are born of God, John writes, then naturally we will also love one another (1 John 2:10–11, 3:10–15, 4:7–21; 2 John 1:4–6; 3 John 1:5–8); hatred for other believers, as John explains in each of these passages, is a sign that we have not yet been born of God. Again, it isn't that anyone will love their brothers and sisters perfectly (1 John 1:6, 8, 10) but that ongoing, unchecked, unrepentant lovelessness is not a possibility for anyone who has been born of God (1 John 3:4–15, 4:7–21; 3 John 1:11)

And John takes love seriously—he does not let us off easily here. John insists that the children of God must be willing to lay down their lives for one another (1 John 3:16), but for those of us who will never be asked to die in a literal sense for another believer, John gives us a blunt and challenging test: "But whoever has the livelihood of the world and sees his brother having need and closes his heart from him, how does the love of God abide in him?" (1 John

3:17). In fact, in the measure that we serve one another, we serve God himself (3 John 1:6).

Here is what this means for our discipleship: Jesus died to make us part of his church, not for us to remain as isolated individuals. Remember that at the very beginning of this letter, John wrote, "what we have seen and heard, we bear witness also to you, that also you may have fellowship with us. And our fellowship is with the Father and with his Son Jesus Christ. And these things we write, that our joy may be filled" (1 John 1:3–4). John's letter calls us to enjoy full fellowship with the church so that "if we walk in the light just as he is in the light, we have fellowship with one other and the blood of Jesus his Son cleanses us from all sin" (1 John 1:7). We are called to support and stand with one another—especially those who are called to special ministries for the sake of the name—so that we may all be considered "fellow-workers for the truth" (3 John 1:8).

Discipleship cannot happen outside the context of the church. We cannot really have Jesus while rejecting his church, because a core part of what it means to be a Christ follower is to enjoy fellowship in the community of other believers. Obedience to Jesus means sharing in one another's joys and sorrows, serving one another whenever anyone has a need, sitting together regularly at the feet of Jesus to learn from his word, and comparing notes with one another about what our Lord is teaching us.

Joining a local church is not the process through which we receive eternal life—Jesus alone gives life through faith in his name (1 John 5:12–13). But, membership and active participation in the local church is the only way we can fulfill the commandment Jesus has given us from the beginning, that we should love one another (1 John 2:7, 3:11; 2 John 1:4–6). Why? Because love cannot happen in the abstract. Love can only happen when we care for the brothers and sisters whom we actually see in our midst (1 John 4:20; 3 John 1:5–8).

Little children, let us not love in word or in tongue but in work and in truth.

A PRIMER ON DISCIPLESHIP

And now we come to the end of John's primer on discipleship. Brothers and sisters, be encouraged—the day is coming when Jesus will appear, and we will be like him, for we will see him as he is! We have nothing to fear, for the perfect love of God we have in Christ through the anointing of the Holy Spirit drives out fear.

So as we wait for his coming, let us practice righteousness as he is righteous. Seek to know God through his word. Repent from your sins. Believe the gospel. Love one another, just as God has loved you. These things are simple enough on paper, but we have a lifetime's worth of growth ahead of us as we persevere forward, until Jesus returns and completes the good work he has begun in us.

In the meantime, do not love the world or the things of the world. Beware the antichrists who preach to you that Jesus is not the Son of God, as well as the false prophets who try to undercut the full humanity of Jesus. For we know the Son of God came, and he has given to us understanding so that we know the True One, and we are in the True One, in his Son Jesus Christ. This one is true God and eternal life.

Little children, keep yourselves from idols.

Notes

Introduction

1. Gregory the Great, *Moralia, or Commentary on the Book of the Blessed Job*, trans. James. J. O'Donnell, §4. www9.georgetown.edu/faculty/jod/texts/moralia1

Chapter 1: Truth (1 John 1:1-4)

1. R. C. H. Lenski, *The Interpretation of the Epistles of St. Peter, St. John, and St. Jude* (Minneapolis: Augsburg, 1966), 376.

2. Again, most translations use the word *with* in John 1:1, but the Greek word is actually *pros*, just like in 1 John 1:2.

3. George Smeaton, *The Doctrine of the Holy Spirit* (Edinburgh: Banner of Truth Trust, 1974), 267.

4. Cyprian of Carthage, *The Lapsed; The Unity of the Catholic Church*, trans. Maurice Bévenot, in *Ancient Christian Writers*, no. 25 (New York: Newman Press, 1956), 48–49.

Chapter 2: Gospel (1 John 1:5-2:6)

1. A libertine is the name given to Christians who sin freely because they over–emphasize Christian liberty. People who make this mistake are also called antinomians, from the two Greek words *anti* (in place of) and *nomos* (law).

2. *Memoir and Remains of the Rev. Robert Murray M'Cheyne,* ed. Andrew Bonar (London: Dundee, 1845), 254.

CHAPTER 3: GROWTH (1 JOHN 2:7–14)

1. See Matthew 22:34–40 and Mark 12:28–34.

2. This outline is adapted from Warren Wiersbe, *The Bible Exposition Commentary, New Testament,* vol. 2 (Colorado Springs: Victor, 1989), 485–91.

3. John Calvin, *Commentaries on the Catholic Epistles,* vol. 22, trans. John Owen (Grand Rapids: Baker, 2005), 181. See e.g., Lenski, *Interpretation of the Epistles,* 417; Wiersbe, *Bible Exposition Commentary,* 495.

CHAPTER 4: PERSEVERANCE (1 JOHN 2:15–27)

1. Augustine, "Sermon 335C: The Sermon of the Blessed Bishop Augustine on the Feast of a Martyr," in *Augustine: Political Writings,* ed. E. M. Atkins and R. J. Dodaro (New York: Cambridge UP, 2001), 59.

2. E.g., "pride in riches" (New Revised Standard Version), or "pride in possessions" (ESV).

3. Lenski, *Interpretation of the Epistles,* 426.

4. Thomas Chalmers, "Discourse IX. The Expulsive Power of a New Affection," in *The Works of Thomas Chalmers,* vol. 6 (New York: Robert Carter, 1840), 209.

5. Lenski, *Interpretation of the Epistles,* 427.

6. Chalmers, "Discourse IX," 209.

CHAPTER 5: HOPE (1 JOHN 2:28–3:10)

1. Dietrich Bonhoeffer, *The Cost of Discipleship* (New York: Touchstone, 1995), 89.

2. 1 John 2:6, 10, 14, 17, 19, 24 (3x), 27 (2x), 28; 3:6, 9, 14, 15, 17, 24 (2x); 4:12, 13, 15, 16.

Chapter 6: Righteousness (1 John 3:11–24)

1. Donald Burdick, *The Letters of John the Apostle: An In-Depth Commentary* (Chicago: Moody, 1985), 267.

2. Ibid., 273; John Stott, *The Epistles of John: An Introduction and Commentary* (Grand Rapids: Eerdmans, 1964), 147.

3. John Calvin, *Commentaries on the First Epistle of John*, in *Calvin Commentaries*, vol. 22 (Grand Rapids: Baker, 2005), 222–23.

4. C. S. Lewis, *Mere Christianity* (New York: HarperCollins, 2001), 210, 213.

5. Calvin, *Commentaries on the First Epistle of John*, 224.

6. Stott, *Epistles of John*, 149.

Chapter 7: Discernment (1 John 4:1–6)

1. Chris Anderson, *The Long Tail: Why the Future of Business Is Selling Less of More* (New York: Hyperion, 2006).

2. Gregory of Nazianzus, "Letter 101," in *Nicene and Post-Nicene Fathers*, 2nd series, vol. 7, trans. Charles G. Browne and James E. Swallow (Grand Rapids: Eerdmans, 1955), 440.

3. *A Select Library of Nicene and Post-Nicene Fathers of the Christian Church*, 2nd series, vol. 14, trans. Philip Schaff and Henry Wace (New York: Charles Scribner's Sons, 1905), 264.

4. Burdick, *Letters of John*, 295.

5. Ibid., 298.

6. Stott, *Epistles of John*, 157.

Chapter 8: Love (1 John 4:7–21)

1. Lenski, *Interpretation of the Epistles*, 495.

2. Additionally, John made emphatic use of the article *the*

in 4:3: "every spirit that does not confess *the* Jesus having come in the flesh is not from God" to differentiate the having-come-in-flesh Jesus from the various false versions of Jesus promoted by the prophets of the spirit of error.

3. C. S. Lewis, *The Problem of Pain* (New York: HarperCollins, 1996), 39.

4. Colin Kruse, *The Letters of John*, Pillar New Testament Commentary (Grand Rapids: Eerdmans, 2000), 163.

CHAPTER 9: FAITH (1 JOHN 5:1–12)

1. Stott, *Epistles of John*, 172.

2. John Murray, *Redemption Accomplished and Applied* (London: Banner of Truth Trust, 1961), 103.

3. Burdick, *Letters of John*, 372.

CHAPTER 10: PRAYER (1 JOHN 5:13–17)

1. Stott, *Epistles of John*, 185.

2. Jeremiah 7:16–18, 11:14, 14:11; see also Kruse, *Letters of John*, 193.

3. Lenski, *Interpretation of the Epistles*, 534–35, emphasis added.

CHAPTER 11: ETERNAL LIFE (1 JOHN 5:18–21)

1. Burdick, *Letters of John*, 393.

2. Stott, *Epistles of John*, 194.

3. Appian, *The Civil Wars*, book 1, §120.

4. Lenski, *Interpretation of the Epistles*, 544–45.

CHAPTER 12: THE CASE STUDY OF THE ELECT LADY (2 JOHN)

1. The only other New Testament letter that does not

contain a greeting at the beginning of the letter is Hebrews, but Hebrews does contain a few greetings at the very end of the letter, while 1 John does not include greetings from the author to specific recipients at any point.

2. Kruse, *Letters of John*, 205.

3. The first four of these deviations are found in Stott, *Epistles of John*, 203–5.

4. Lenski, *Interpretation of the Epistles*, 559–60.

5. Donald Burdick writes, "This double emphasis [on truth and love] sets the tone for the entire letter as John proceeds to show the careful balance in which these two elements of the Christian life must be held." Burdick, *Letters of John*, 431. In this chapter, I draw heavily from Burdick's extended section on the relationship between truth and love (pp. 431–33).

6. Stott, *Epistles of John*, 199.

CHAPTER 13: THE CASE STUDY OF GAIUS AND DIOTREPHES (3 JOHN)

1. Stott, *Epistles of John*, 198, 213.

2. Kruse, *Letters of John*, 220.

3. Burdick, *Letters of John*, 460–61.

4. John Piper, *Let the Nations Be Glad! The Supremacy of God in Missions*, 2nd ed. (Grand Rapids: Baker Academic, 2003), 17.

5. Lenski, *Interpretation of the Epistles*, 577.

6. E.g., Stott, *Epistles of John*, 224–25; Burdick, *Letters of John*, 444; Kruse, *Letters of John*, 226.

7. E.g., Lenski, *Interpretation of the Epistles*, 588; Burdick, *Letters of John*, 463.

8. Burdick, *Letters of John*, 454.

Made in the USA
Charleston, SC
04 October 2014